Irish Soups
& Breads

Irish Soups & Breads

Nuala Cullen

Gill & Macmillan

Gill & Macmillan Ltd
Hume Avenue, Park West
Dublin 12
with associated companies throughout the world
www.gillmacmillan.ie
© Nuala Cullen 2001
0 7171 3154 8

Index compiled by Cover To Cover
Illustrations by Eva Byrne
Design by Slick Fish Design
Print origination by Carole Lynch
Printed by ColourBooks, Dublin

This book is typeset in 9/14 pt Avenir.

*The paper used in this book is made from the wood pulp
of managed forests. For every tree felled, at least one tree is
planted, thereby renewing natural resources.*

A catalogue record for this book is available
from the British Library.

3 5 4

Contents

Soups

Introduction

Since man first learned to boil his meat in troughs heated by hot stones, soup — or broth — has been part of the diet. It has served many functions in different societies and at different times, from a breakfast drink to a standing pottage, but in our society it did not take its present place as an introduction to the meal until the eighteenth century.

In the nineteenth century, soup in Ireland even developed political connotations. Catholics who were starving during the terrible famine years of the 1840s, and who changed

their religion in exchange for sustenance from Protestant societies, were called 'soupers'. But perhaps the most famous soup of that unhappy period was created by Alexis Soyer, the philanthropic and inventive chef de cuisine of the Reform Club in London.

Soyer set up his soup kitchen, equipped with his specially invented stove and excellent but controversial recipe, on the parade ground of the Royal Barracks in Dublin, now the National Museum, and in the period between 6 April and 14 August 1847, 1,147,279 rations were distributed to the needy, an average of 8,750 daily. The famous chef returned to the Reform Club with his reputation much enhanced and a beautiful memento in the shape of a silver snuff box presented to him at a dinner given in his honour in Dublin.

While in Dublin Soyer, in response to requests, published a booklet entitled, *The Poor Man's Regenerator*, containing economical recipes for soups and stews, in which he implored people to use the outsides of vegetables instead of throwing them away. In this he was, as in many other things relating to nutrition, in advance of his time.

Happily today we can take a more relaxed view of soup, eating it for pleasure rather than mere survival. Though many of the recipes included here are from a traditional background, they have been updated to eliminate the hours of cooking once considered necessary, even for lettuce and pea soups, and reflect a lighter, fresher and healthier approach to soup-making.

Soup is infinitely versatile and suited to every occasion, from the warming winter family lunch to a summer evening dinner party, and the selection of recipes which follows will, I hope, be enjoyed.

The quantities given in each recipe are for six, unless otherwise stated.

Stocks

Good stocks are the foundation of good soup and should be carefully prepared with ingredients which are absolutely fresh and chosen with care.

It is not a good idea to put leftovers of all descriptions into the stockpot, leaving it to boil for hours — this simply produces a cloudy liquid with a tired and indeterminate flavour. Instead, choose the required ingredients especially for each stock and don't cook for longer than necessary.

It is unrealistic to expect that the necessary stocks will always be to hand, or that there will always be time to make them. For such occasions stock cubes can be used, remembering that they are already salted (to my taste, over-salted), so it is best when making soup not to add salt until last, as in fact it may not be necessary.

Stock cubes vary greatly in strength and quality, and in the number of additives they contain. There are organic, largely additive-free stock cubes on the market, usually to be found in health food stores and some supermarkets and it is worthwhile experimenting with a few different brands to find the flavours you like. For light vegetable soups, where you want the flavour of the principal ingredient to dominate, use only half the recommended number of cubes.

When adding stock to soup ingredients it is a good idea to hold back a little, to be added later when the soup is almost ready, as it may not be required. It is easier to thin a soup than thicken one if there is too much liquid.

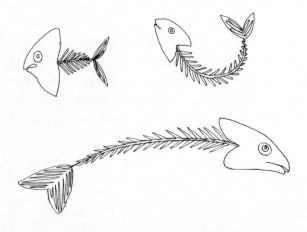

FISH STOCK

Most fishmongers will be happy to part with the bones and trimmings of white fish when you are making a purchase. Just be sure they are absolutely fresh.

- 1.5 kg/3 lb white fish bones or trimmings
- 1 large onion
- 1 stick celery
- 50 g/2 oz/¾ cup sliced mushrooms
- 1 leek
- 2 litres/ 3½ pints/10 cups water
- 1 tablespoon lemon juice
- bay leaf, sprig thyme, parsley
- 1 large glass white wine or dry cider
- 1 teaspoon peppercorns

Put the chopped vegetables in a large saucepan with the butter, cover and sweat the vegetables for 5 minutes. Add the rinsed fish bones, wine, peppercorns, lemon juice and herbs. Cover with the cold water and bring to the boil. Lower the heat and simmer gently for about 30 minutes, skimming once or twice. Strain the stock through a large sieve, cool quickly and transfer to the fridge as soon a possible. The stock can be kept in the fridge for a few days, but for longer storage transfer to the freezer.

CHICKEN STOCK

- 1.125 kg/2 lb 8 oz chicken carcasses or wings etc.
- 350 g/12 oz/2½ cups carrots
- 2 sticks celery
- 2 onions
- 2 leeks
- bay leaf, sprig thyme
- a few peppercorns
- 2 litres/3½ pints/10 cups water
- 2 cloves
- 1 glass white wine, optional

Rinse the chicken carcasses in cold water and put into a large saucepan. Add the other ingredients, cover with the water, bring quickly to the boil, stirring well for a few minutes and skimming when necessary. Cover, lower the heat and simmer gently, with the water barely shivering, and skimming from time to time, for about an hour and a half. Strain the stock, cool as quickly as possible and chill. The stock can be kept for a few days in the fridge, but for longer storage transfer to the freezer.

For a stronger flavour the carcasses can be roasted in a hot oven for 30 minutes before making the stock.

VEGETABLE STOCK

- 2–3 leeks
- 2–3 cloves garlic
- 2 sticks celery
- 150 g/5 oz/1½ cups sliced mushrooms
- 350 g/12 oz carrots
- 225 g/8 oz/2 cups onions
- 2 tablespoons olive oil
- 1 teaspoon peppercorns
- 2 tablespoons lemon juice
- 1 glass cider, optional
- 2 litres/3½ pints/10 cups water

Heat the oil in a large saucepan, add the roughly chopped vegetables and sweat for 10 minutes. Cover with the water, add the lemon juice and cider and simmer very gently for an hour. Strain, cool as quickly as possible and transfer to the fridge. The stock can be kept in the fridge for a few days, but for longer storage keep in the freezer.

PULSES AND NUT SOUPS

CURRIED TURNIP AND LENTIL SOUP

These homely and traditional ingredients are given a lift by the curry in this comforting and substantial soup.

- 350 g/12 oz/2 cups prepared turnip
- 175 g/6 oz/1 cup green or brown lentils, soaked 1–2 hours
- 1.2 litres/2 pints/5¼ cups vegetable stock
- 1 large onion, finely chopped
- 2 tablespoons finely chopped parsley
- 1 large carrot
- 1 tablespoon olive oil
- 1 tablespoon mild curry powder or paste
- salt and black pepper

Cut the peeled turnip and carrot into small cubes. Melt the oil in a large saucepan, add the onion and cook gently until the onion is soft. Add the vegetables and curry powder and cook, stirring, for about 5 minutes until the oil is absorbed. Add the lentils and the stock and cook until the vegetables are tender and the lentils cooked, about 40 to 50 minutes, depending on how long the lentils have been soaking.

Check the seasoning, adding a little more curry powder if required. Stir in the chopped parsley just before serving.

The soup can be puréed in a blender if a smooth consistency is preferred.

WALNUT SOUP

This soup can be made at any time of year, but winter is best, when the new season's nuts are fresh — a perfect dinner party soup, not too filling and quick to make.

- 175 g/6 oz/1½ cups shelled walnuts
- 1 litre/1¾ pints/5 cups strong home-made chicken stock
- 1 large clove garlic
- salt and freshly ground black pepper
- 150 g/¼ pint/½ cup cream
- parsley or chives to garnish
- nutmeg or mace

Crush or blend the walnuts and garlic to a smooth paste, adding a little stock to help it along. Blend in the rest of the stock, add the cream and season well. Bring to the boil, lower the heat and simmer gently for 4–5 minutes. Season to taste, grate a very little mace or nutmeg into the soup and scatter the herbs over the top.

CELERY AND ALMOND SOUP

- 275 g/10 oz/3 cups celery
- 100 g/4 oz/1 cup ground almonds
- 175 g/6 oz/2½ cups leeks
- 50 g/2 oz/4 tablespoons butter
- 1 litre/1¾ pints/5 cups light chicken stock
- 1 tablespoon chopped chervil
- 150 ml/¼ pint/½ cup cream
- 2 teaspoons ground coriander
- salt and black pepper

Clean and finely chop the leeks and celery, including any green celery leaves. Sauté in the butter until soft without browning. Add the chervil and the ground almonds and stir together for a few moments. Gradually add the hot stock and simmer gently until the celery is tender, about 15–20 minutes.

Check the seasoning, add coriander to taste and then add the cream. For a rich creamy soup purée the mixture in two batches in a blender or food processor, or if a little texture is preferred, just purée half the soup. Return to the saucepan to reheat. Garnish with chopped chervil or green celery leaves.

SPLIT PEA AND BACON SOUP

Yellow split peas have an earthy taste all their own, which contrasts nicely with the bacon.

- 225 g/8 oz/1¼ cups yellow split peas
- 4–5 rashers streaky bacon
- 1 potato, peeled and cubed
- 2 cloves garlic
- 1 carrot
- 1 stick celery
- 1 small onion
- 1 tablespoon oil
- 1.2 litres/2 pints/5½ cups water or light vegetable stock
- 4 tablespoons cream
- teaspoon ground cumin
- salt and black pepper

Rinse the peas in cold water and soak overnight. Rinse again in cold water and drain.

Peel and roughly chop the potato, carrot, celery, onion and garlic and put with the peas into a large saucepan. Pour in the water or stock, bring to the boil and cover with a lid. Simmer gently until the peas are soft. This will take about 40 minutes, depending on the peas and how long they have been soaking.

Purée the soup in a blender, return to the saucepan and taste for seasoning. Mix the cumin with the cream and stir in well. If the soup is too thick, add a little more stock or water.

While the peas are cooking, heat the oil in a frying pan and sauté the finely chopped bacon very slowly until it is golden brown and crisp, then drain on kitchen paper.

Reheat the soup and serve in deep plates with the bacon sprinkled on top.

CHESTNUT SOUP

A lovely soup with something of the warm and earthy colours of autumn.

To prepare the chestnuts, score them across on the rounded side, and either put them in a low oven (160°C/330°F/Gas 3) for 20 minutes or drop them into boiling water and boil for about 10 minutes. Take them out a few at a time, squeeze hard to crack the shell, then with a small sharp knife remove the inner and outer skins.

Canned unsweetened chestnut purée or canned whole chestnuts can also be used.

- 350 g/¾ lb prepared chestnuts
- 100 g/¼ lb/½ cup green lentils
- 3 streaky bacon rashers
- 2 medium onions
- 3 cloves garlic
- 2 sticks celery, with leaves
- 1 carrot
- 50 g/2 oz/4 tablespoons butter
- 1.2 litres/2 pints/5½ cups chicken or vegetable stock
- 150 ml/¼ pint/½ cup cream
- salt and black pepper

Put the finely chopped bacon, onions and garlic in a large saucepan with the butter and sauté until the bacon is cooked and the onions are soft. Put aside the celery leaves for the garnish and finely chop the celery and carrot, add to the saucepan and cook for 3–4 minutes.

Put the chestnuts in a blender with a little of the stock, purée to a smooth cream and pour into the saucepan. Add the lentils and the remainder of the stock and simmer until the lentils are soft. The soup can now be puréed, or if a little texture is preferred, reserve one or two cupfuls of the soup, purée the remainder and return to the reserved soup. Season well, reheat and serve with a little cream in each bowl and the chopped celery leaves sprinkled over the top.

PUY LENTIL AND BROCCOLI SOUP

Puy lentils are those tiny whole lentils — they have an excellent flavour, don't collapse during cooking and have a good appearance in the finished dish. Any brown or green lentil can be used instead.

- 225 g/½ lb/1⅓ cups Puy lentils
- 400 g/12 oz/3 good cups broccoli
- 1 large Spanish onion
- 2–3 cloves garlic
- 5 strips smoked streaky bacon
- 1.2 litres/2 pints/5½ cups vegetable stock
- 1 glass red wine
- 2 tablespoons olive oil
- 1 carrot, grated
- 1 sprig thyme
- lemon juice
- salt and black pepper
- 2–3 tablespoons chopped parsley

Wash the broccoli, then cut off the green florets into small spoonable pieces. Peel the thick stalks, starting at the stalk end and pulling upwards, then chop into small cubes. Blanch the florets in boiling salted water until just tender but still crisp, about 2–3 minutes. Drain and run under cold water.

Peel the onion and garlic, chop them quite finely, then cook slowly over a medium heat in a large saucepan with the chopped bacon until the onions are soft and the bacon is crisp. Pour in the red wine and bubble hard for a moment. Now add the lentils which have been washed and looked over carefully for little stones. Add in the hot stock, the carrot, broccoli stalks, thyme, lots of black pepper and a spoonful of lemon juice.

Cover and simmer gently until the lentils are tender, about 30–40 minutes, then take out the thyme. Stir in the broccoli florets and the parsley, simmering gently for a few moments to reheat, and adding a little more stock if the soup is too thick. Check the seasoning — it may need salt.

Serve very hot, swirling a spoonful of olive oil into each bowl, with lots of good bread and butter on hand.

BARLEY SOUP

Barley soup has a past stretching back to antiquity and there are innumerable variations on the theme of herbs, vegetables and barley — here is just one of them. It keeps well in the fridge for a day or two and it's a comforting soup to have on hand.

- 75 g/3 oz/½ cup pearl barley
- 1 large onion
- 2 carrots
- 2 sticks celery
- sprig oregano or marjoram
- 50 g/2 oz/4 tablespoons butter
- 1.2 litres/2 pints/5½ cups stock or water
- salt and black pepper
- finely chopped parsley to garnish

Soak the barley in water overnight. Melt the butter in a large saucepan and cook the finely chopped onion until soft, but not browned.

Cut the washed celery into very fine dice and grate the carrot on the coarse side of a grater. Add to the saucepan with the oregano and cook for a few moments until the butter is absorbed. Add the stock and the barley, cover and cook very gently until the barley is soft, about 40–50 minutes. Stir from time to time as the barley is inclined to stick to the bottom of the saucepan when it begins to swell. Season well and garnish with the chopped parsley.

This soup improves if made the day before it is required but may need a little more stock as the barley continues to swell slightly.

Croûtons made from barley bread (page 105), cubed and fried in butter, provide an interesting contrast with the tender barley.

FISH SOUPS

SMOKED SALMON SOUP

A delicately flavoured creamy soup.

- 225 g/8 oz smoked salmon
- 175 g/6 oz/1½ cups fennel, finely sliced
- 175 g/6 oz/1 cup leek
- 25 g/1 oz/2 tablespoons butter
- 300 ml/½ pint/1 cup cream
- 900 ml/1½ pints/3½ cups fish stock
- 100 g/4 oz /1 cup cubed potato
- lime juice
- 3 teaspoons paprika
- 6 teaspoons olive oil
- black pepper

Melt the butter in a large saucepan. Add the cleaned and chopped leek, the fennel, a teaspoon of paprika and the peeled and cubed potato. Cook gently for 2 or 3 minutes, then add the stock and simmer gently for 20 minutes. Take the soup off the heat and leave to cool slightly, then add the chopped smoked salmon and lime juice to taste. Leave to infuse for a few minutes, then purée the mixture in a food processor or blender until completely smooth and return to the saucepan. Check the seasoning, add the cream and reheat gently, but don't allow it to boil or the soup will curdle and separate. Should this happen, push through a sieve and reheat gently, again without boiling.

When serving, mix together 6 teaspoons of olive oil and 3 teaspoons of paprika until smooth, then dribble a teaspoonful of the mixture in a circle on to each serving.

CRAB SOUP WITH SAFFRON

Fresh crab is such a delicacy it is best eaten as simply as possible, but if there is a little surplus try this classic soup.

- 175 g/6 oz freshly cooked crabmeat
- 6 large spring onions
- pinch saffron strands
- 1 clove garlic
- 2 teaspoons chopped fresh marjoram
- 50 g/1 oz/2 tablespoons butter
- 1 tablespoon flour
- 900 ml/1½ pints/3½ cups fish or light chicken stock
- 1 tablespoon long grain rice
- 1 tablespoon grated lemon zest
- 150 ml/¼ pint/½ cup cream
- 4 tablespoons dry vermouth or sherry, optional
- 1 tablespoon chopped herbs to garnish

Soak the saffron in a half-cup of water for a few minutes. Cook the finely chopped spring onions, garlic and marjoram in the butter until soft. Mix in the flour and stir well for a few moments. Add the hot stock, stirring well until it thickens slightly, then add the rice, vermouth, lemon zest and saffron, with its water, and simmer gently until the rice is soft.

Add the cream, bring back to a gentle simmer, season well, then stir in the crab, heating gently, without boiling, for 2 or 3 minutes until the crab is hot. Serve garnished with the herbs.

SMOKED HADDOCK SOUP
WITH MUSHROOMS

- 575 g/1¼ lb smoked haddock or cod
- 225 g/½ lb/2½ cups mushrooms, sliced
- 1 small onion, finely chopped
- ½ lemon
- 600 ml/1 pint/2 cups water
- 425 ml/¾ pint/1½ cups milk
- 25 g/1 oz/2 tablespoons butter
- 1 tablespoon flour
- black pepper and a bay leaf
- parsley, finely chopped

Bring the water to the boil in a large saucepan, add the bay leaf, a squeeze of lemon juice and a few grinds of black pepper. Cut the fish into large pieces and poach until cooked, about 5 minutes, then remove to a plate, reserving the liquid. Discard the bay leaf.

In another pan melt the butter and sauté the finely chopped onion and the sliced mushrooms until soft. Mix in the flour, stirring well until the flour is cooked, then gradually add the hot milk and enough of the reserved stock to give the desired consistency. Taste for seasoning then return the fish to the soup and reheat gently.

Serve in deep soup plates with plenty of finely chopped parsley and grated lemon rind, or pats of herb butter.

SEAFOOD CHOWDER
WITH SAFFRON

A classic chowder with a hint of saffron.

- 375 g/¾ lb cod or other white fish
- 100 g/4 oz salmon
- 450 g/1 lb mixed mussels and prawns
- 4 pieces streaky bacon, cut in fine strips
- 1 each carrot, leek, onion, celery
- 2 large potatoes
- 900 ml/1½ pints/3¾ cups water or fish stock
- 300 ml/½ pint/1¼ cups cream
- 7 g/½ oz carrageen moss,* optional
- 150 g/2 oz/4 tablespoons butter
- 1 large tablespoon flour
- 1 pinch saffron
- salt and black pepper
- 1 tablespoon finely chopped parsley

Heat the cream, put in the saffron and leave to infuse.

Bring the water or fish stock to a boil and poach the cod and salmon for 5 minutes. Lift out, carefully remove any bones or skin, flake the fish and set aside. If the mussels and prawns are uncooked, poach them in the stock for 3 minutes or so until all the mussels have opened, then remove and shell the prawns, discard any mussels that have not opened, and set aside. Strain the stock carefully and reserve.

Melt the butter in the saucepan and cook the bacon until crisp. Remove and drain on kitchen paper. Add the peeled and chopped vegetables to the saucepan, tossing around to absorb the butter for a few moments. Stir in the flour, mix well, then gradually add the strained stock, stirring until smooth. Cover and cook gently until the vegetables are tender, about 10–15 minutes. Pour in the cream and saffron and simmer gently for a few minutes.

Taste for seasoning, return the fish and shellfish to the saucepan and reheat gently.

Serve in deep soup plates scattered with the bacon and parsley, with freshly baked brown soda bread and lots of butter.

*Carrageen: reddish purple sea vegetable, also known as Irish moss, rich in calcium and other essential vitamins and minerals.

OYSTER SOUP

In this recipe the oysters are briefly poached in a light and creamy stock — ideal for those who prefer their oysters cooked.

- ■ 12–16 oysters
- ■ 50 g/2 oz/4 tablespoons butter
- ■ 2 tablespoons very finely chopped onion
- ■ 2 tablespoons very finely chopped celery
- ■ 600 ml/1 pint/2½ cups milk
- ■ 150 ml/¼ pint/½ cup cream
- ■ 150 ml/¼ pint/½ cup dry white wine
- ■ 1 tablespoon flour
- ■ 2 tablespoons finely chopped chives or parsley
- ■ black pepper and a pinch of cayenne, or Tabasco
- ■ 1 lemon

Open the oysters, being careful to preserve the juice, and put them in the fridge.

In a saucepan melt the butter and sauté the vegetables carefully, without browning. Sprinkle in the flour and stir until it is cooked, then add the wine, the strained oyster liquid and the milk, stirring until the mixture thickens slightly. Taste for seasoning and add a little cayenne or Tabasco to taste.

When ready to serve, add the cream, bring to the boil and simmer for 5 minutes or so to reduce slightly, then add the oysters, bring back to the boil and cook for less than a minute until they plump up and their edges begin to curl. Remove from the heat and serve immediately garnished with finely chopped chives or parsley, and lemon wedges.

SALMON AND LEEK SOUP

Leeks and salmon seem to have a natural affinity, nicely demonstrated in this soup. Chervil can take the place of tarragon if a more delicate flavour is preferred. Garnish with little pastry fleurons (page 84), lemon wedges and a leaf or two of tarragon, or finely chopped chives.

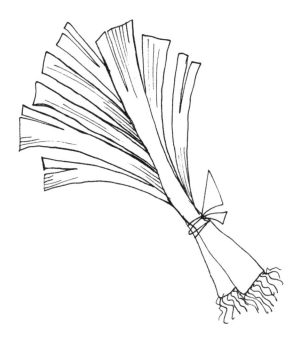

- 175 g/10 oz salmon
- 3 medium leeks, thinly sliced
- 50 g/2 oz/4 tablespoons butter
- 1 tablespoon flour
- 1 glass white wine
- 1 litre/ 1¾ pints/5 cups fish or light chicken stock
- 150 ml/¼ pint/½ cup cream
- 4–5 leaves fresh tarragon or pinch dried chervil
- salt and black pepper
- lemon slices and fleurons to garnish

Melt the butter in a large saucepan, add the tarragon and the thinly sliced leeks, cover and cook gently, about 5 or 6 minutes, until they have softened but still retain a good green colour.

While the leeks are cooking bring the stock to a boil and gently poach the salmon for 4–5 minutes, until just cooked. Lift out and carefully remove the bones and skin, break gently into flakes and set aside.

Pour the wine into the saucepan with the leeks and bubble hard for a minute or two to concentrate the flavour. Now add the flour, stirring well to cook a little, then gradually add the hot stock, stirring until the soup has thickened slightly. Taste for seasoning, then stir in the cream, simmering for 2 or 3 minutes to reduce slightly.

When ready to serve, reheat the soup, add the flaked salmon, allow a few moments for the salmon to heat up, and serve immediately, garnished with the lemon wedges and fleurons.

MAIN COURSE SOUPS

OLD FASHIONED KIDNEY SOUP

Kidney soup used to be the grand staple of every hotel and restaurant menu in the past — over-exposure and bad cooking caused its undeserved near extinction. It's a great winter soup and easy to make. Lambs' kidneys are cheap and easy to find. Cut them in two and soak them in vinegared salted water for an hour or two for a more delicate flavour.

- 4–5 lambs' kidneys
- 4 tablespoons butter
- 1.2 litres/2 pints/5¼ cups chicken stock
- 1 large onion
- 1 small white turnip
- 3 carrots
- 3 sticks celery
- sprig fresh thyme or pinch of dried
- ½ teaspoon mace
- 1 large tablespoon flour
- 2 teaspoons curry powder
- Worcester sauce
- chopped parsley

Melt the butter in a large saucepan and gently cook the onions until transparent. While they are cooking, take the kidneys from their casing of fat, peel off the fine membrane and slice them in half. Cut out the white core with scissors. Chop them into small pieces and toss them in the flour. If they have been soaking in vinegared water, dry them first. Add the kidneys to the onions and stir about for a few moments to brown them. Next add the finely chopped vegetables, the herbs and mace.

Pour in the hot stock, taste for salt and cook gently for about 45 minutes until the kidneys are tender. Purée in a blender or food processor and return to the pan. A little curry powder and a dash or two of Worcester sauce can be added to sharpen the flavour.

If a little texture is preferred, a few pieces of kidney can be removed before blending, chopped finely and returned to the finished soup. Add a generous sprinkle of chopped parsley when serving.

A glass of not too dry sherry, say, an Amontillado, is just the thing with this soup.

BEEF SOUP WITH FLUFFY DUMPLINGS

This slow-cooking dish is more of a stew than a soup, but whatever the category it is a comforting dish. The dumplings are on page 83.

- 675 g/1½ lb rib beef
- 1 leek, finely sliced
- 2 each carrots, celery sticks and onions, chopped
- ¼ teaspoon caraway seeds

- 175 ml/6 fl oz/1 cup Guinness stout
- 900 ml/1½ pints/4½ cups strong beef or chicken stock
- 225 g/½ lb/1½ cups small button mushrooms
- 3 tablespoons tiny peeled onions, optional
- 2 sprigs thyme and a bay leaf
- 2 tablespoons flour
- 2 tablespoons oil
- 2 tablespoons butter
- 2–3 tablespoons chopped parsley
- salt and pepper

Chop the beef into fairly small cubes, toss in the flour and brown lightly in a tablespoon of oil — it is easier to brown the meat if it is at room temperature. Remove the meat to a plate, add another tablespoon of oil to the saucepan and brown the onions and leek. Return the beef to the saucepan, add the carrots and celery, the seasoning, herbs, stock and stout. Simmer very slowly for about an hour, then add the mushrooms and small onions and continue to cook for another 45 minutes or so, or until the meat is really tender. Remove the bay leaf and thyme sprigs.

While the meat is cooking, make the dumplings. Add them to the soup about half an hour before the end of the cooking period, letting them sit on top of the soup so that they cook in the steam, as too much heat may cause the egg in the dumplings to toughen. Turn them over gently once or twice with a large spoon.

Serve in deep plates generously sprinkled with parsley, with plenty of brown bread and butter on the side.

If the soup liquid is not thick enough, mash a tablespoon of flour into a tablespoon of butter and add in tiny pieces to the saucepan, stirring well until the liquid thickens slightly. This process can be repeated if necessary.

SCOTCH BROTH

Originally made with mutton, this old traditional soup has stood the test of time. Nowadays it is made with lamb and cooks in half the time, but it is still as comforting and warming as ever.

- 675 g/1½ lb neck of mutton, or shoulder
- 2 tablespoons pearl barley, optional
- 2 carrots

- 2 onions
- 2 sticks celery
- 1.2 litres/2 pints/5½ cups vegetable or chicken stock
- 2 small white turnips or thick slice swede turnip
- 1 tablespoon olive oil
- salt, pepper, bouquet garni and parsley

Soak the barley overnight, or for several hours. Chop the onions finely and the other vegetables into small dice. Cut the meat into small cubes, removing as much fat as possible.

Heat the oil in a large saucepan, lightly brown the meat and the onions. Pour in the hot stock, add salt, pepper, the bouquet garni, the barley and any celery leaves, and simmer for about 30 minutes when the meat should be almost tender.

Add the diced vegetables to the saucepan and cook gently for a further half an hour or so until the meat and barley are tender. If there are no white turnips to be had, a thick slice of yellow turnip can be added, but do not use too much as the flavour is rather dominant.

Remove the bouquet garni and skim off any fat before serving with lots of parsley sprinkled over the top. The soup can be made and chilled overnight, which allows the flavours to develop and the barley to swell, in which case a little more stock may be needed to thin it.

BALNAMOON SKINK

An old Irish soup, this version is adapted from Meg Dod's *Cook and Housewife's Manual*, 1856 edition. Originally a summer soup made during the short pea season, two chickens were required — one to make the stock, the other poached in it and served whole in the tureen!

Skink is an old Scots/Irish word for a stew/soup.

- 2 large or 3 small chicken breasts
- 1.2 litres/2 pints/5½ cups strong, home-made chicken stock
- 1 medium onion, finely chopped
- 5 or 6 scallions (spring onions)
- 2 tablespoons chopped chives
- 100 g/¼ lb/1 large cup fresh peas, or frozen petits pois
- 25 g/1 oz/2 tablespoons butter
- 1 large tablespoon flour
- sprig fresh tarragon or pinch of dried
- 2 eggs
- 150 ml/¼ pint/½ cup cream
- salt and white pepper

Cut the chicken breasts diagonally into thin strips. Heat the butter in a large saucepan and toss the chicken strips in it until lightly browned, then remove to a plate. Add the onion to the pan and cook gently until soft and nicely coloured. Add the flour and stir well for 2 or 3 minutes until it is cooked, then add the hot stock gradually, stirring well and simmering for 5 or 10 minutes.

Add the peas, chives, tarragon and the finely chopped scallions to the soup and season well. When the peas are cooked, put in the chicken and cook for a further 2 or 3 minutes, but don't overcook the chicken. Take the soup off the heat and leave for a few minutes to cool a little. Beat the two eggs in a small bowl with the cream, pour in a ladleful of the soup, stir and return to the saucepan, stirring well until slightly thickened, but do not allow the soup to boil or the eggs will curdle.

Garnish with a few more chives and serve with wholemeal bread.

MULLIGATAWNY SOUP

This soup, and perhaps kedgeree, are among the last of the many nineteenth-century Anglo-Indian dishes to have retained their popularity and represent the beginning of the Western love affair with Indian food.

- 2 tablespoons mild curry powder
- 6 medium onions
- 2 cloves garlic
- 25 g/1 oz/2 tablespoons ground almonds
- 2–3 oz bacon
- 1.2 litres/2 pints/5½ cups chicken stock
- 1 chicken leg or thigh per person, or
  2 large chicken breasts
- 1 lemon, or lemon or mango pickle
- 150 g/4–5 oz long grain rice, boiled
- 3–4 tablespoons cream
- 2 tablespoons finely chopped parsley
- salt

Cut the bacon into small cubes and slice the onions thinly. Heat the oil in a large saucepan and brown the bacon, push to one side and add the chicken pieces, tossing until browned. Next add the onions

and garlic and cook gently until the onions are softened and lightly coloured.

Stir in the curry powder, cook for a moment, then add the stock and simmer gently until the chicken and bacon are cooked. (If using chicken breasts, it is best to cook them whole, remove them as soon as they are cooked, cut into suitable pieces, then return to the soup just before serving, otherwise they are liable to overcook while the soup is simmering.)

When the meat is ready, mix the ground almonds to a paste with cream or a little of the stock and add it to the soup, simmering for about 10 minutes. Add the lemon juice or pickle to taste, check the seasoning, and serve on deep soup plates, handing the rice separately.

Alternatively, the rice can be shaped into timbales, using oiled dariole moulds or small coffee cups, and turned out on to the centre of the soup plates, with the soup gently ladled around them. To do this, rub the insides of the moulds or cups with a few drops of oil and fill with the hot cooked rice, press down lightly, turn upside down on to the warmed soup plates and lift off the moulds. Sprinkle the rice with very finely chopped parsley.

PUMPKIN SOUP

This lovely soup can be served in the pumpkin, if it's not in use as a Hallowe'en lantern, and the addition of two or three sliced chicken breasts makes it into a substantial main course soup. The cleaned pumpkin seeds can be toasted in the oven and served as a snack with drinks.

- 900 g/2 lb uncooked pumpkin flesh
- 2–3 large chicken breasts, thinly sliced
- 2 onions
- 75 g/3 oz/6 tablespoons butter
- 1 tablespoon olive oil
- 2 strips orange peel
- 1 large carrot, grated
- 2 medium potatoes, cubed
- small pinch saffron
- 1.2 litres/2 pints/5½ cups light chicken stock
- nutmeg and ginger
- salt and black pepper

Cut thick slices from a pumpkin, or cut a slice off the top and scrape out the flesh from inside if the pumpkin is to be used later. Set aside the seeds. Spread the pumpkin flesh on a baking tray, dot with half the butter and cover loosely with foil. Bake in a medium oven until tender, 45–50 minutes. (The pumpkin can be cooked in the stock, but the flavour is incomparably better if baked in the oven.) Infuse the saffron in a cupful of milk.

When cooked, allow the pumpkin to cool slightly, discard any skin, then purée the flesh lightly as otherwise it can be rather stringy in the finished soup. There should be about 450 g (1 lb) or a little more.

Heat the remaining butter and the olive oil in a large saucepan and lightly brown the chicken slices, remove and set aside. Add the finely chopped onion, carrot, potato and strips of orange peel and cook slowly until the onion is soft, then add the pumpkin and any buttery juices and stir for a few moments. Add the stock, the saffron with its steeping milk, and season well with black pepper, salt, a quarter-teaspoon of nutmeg and a teaspoon of ginger. Simmer gently for about 20 minutes, returning the chicken to the saucepan to finish cooking for the last 4 or 5 minutes. Check the seasoning and remove the orange peel before serving.

If the pumpkin is to be used as a tureen, don't scrape out too much flesh. The shell should be at least an inch thick. Put the pumpkin on a baking dish and heat it in the oven for about 10 minutes — not longer as it is liable to collapse inwards. Transfer it to a serving dish before pouring in the hot soup and replacing the lid. A little notch can be cut out of the lid to accommodate the handle of the ladle.

A little whipped cream can be handed separately.

PORK AND RED CABBAGE SOUP

A hearty soup made with ready prepared red cabbage. If you want to cook the red cabbage from scratch, slice it as thinly as possible, pour two or three tablespoons of boiling vinegar over it and toss well. Put the cabbage in a deep casserole, season, barely cover it with water and a lid, and bake in a low oven for 2 hours.

- 350–400 g jar cooked red cabbage (not pickled)
- 450 g/1 lb pork steak
- 2 large cooking apples
- 2 large onions
- 2 tablespoons olive oil
- 2 cloves garlic
- 1 tablespoon Dijon mustard
- 2 tablespoons grated fresh ginger
- 1 litre/1¾ pints/5 cups chicken stock
- salt and black pepper

Cut the pork into small pieces and brown well in hot oil in a large saucepan. Push to one side and add the sliced onions and garlic and cook gently until the onions are soft. Add the peeled and sliced apples, the mustard, ginger and the drained red cabbage. Stir well for a few moments, then add the stock and simmer gently until the meat is tender, about 10 or 15 minutes. Season well and serve very hot in deep bowls.

A proportion of the soup, without the meat, can be puréed if a slightly smoother soup is preferred.

COLD SOUPS

ICED PEAR AND
BLUE CHEESE SOUP

A simple soup, perfect for a summer dinner party, which takes no time at all to make.

Serve it in china soup cups garnished with chives and mint, with sesame biscuits (page 85) or cheese straws (page 84).

- 5 medium-size ripe pears
- 1 litre/1¾ pints/5 cups light apple juice
- 100–125 g/4–5 oz Cashel Blue or Roquefort cheese
- 2 tablespoons chopped chives
- 1 clove garlic, peeled
- lime juice
- salt

Peel and core the pears and put in a food processor or blender. Add the crumbled cheese, garlic, the juice of half a lime, a tablespoon of chives and a pint of the apple juice and blend until smooth. Bring the soup to the boil, then cool and chill. This helps to blend in the cheese completely, but it is not essential. Add the remainder of the apple juice, perhaps a little more lime juice to taste, and chill for 2 or 3 hours.

Garnish with spoonfuls of whipped cream, or crème fraîche, chopped chives or mint leaves.

The soup can also be served hot; add a little powdered ginger to taste and pats of blue cheese butter (page 77).

VICHYSSOISE SOUP

Although this classic soup is American, it was invented in 1917 by a Frenchman, Louis Diat, chef de cuisine at the Ritz-Carlton in New York for over forty years. It is so nearly related to our own traditional leek and potato soups that I think we can include it here.

- 4 medium leeks
- 1 medium onion
- 300 g/10 oz/4 medium potatoes
- 750 ml/1¼ pints/3 cups light chicken stock
- 50 g/2 oz/4 tablespoons butter
- 300 ml/½ pint/1 cup cream
- ¼ teaspoon mace

- 2 tablespoons chopped chives
- salt and white pepper

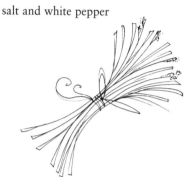

Melt the butter in a large saucepan and gently cook the finely chopped onions and leeks, covered with a lid, for about 10 minutes. Peel the potatoes, slice very thinly and add to the pan, tossing well to absorb the butter. Pour the hot stock over the vegetables and cook, covered, for 15 minutes or so until the potatoes are soft. Purée in a blender and return to the pan. Add the cream and the mace and season to taste. Chill for several hours and serve in small soup cups with the chopped chives scattered on top.

When good freshly cooked prawns are to be had, a nice variation can be made by puréeing a few prawns with a little of the chilled soup, blending this with the rest of the soup and garnishing with a few more prawns in each bowl. A little grated lemon rind can be scattered on top with the chives.

Milk, cream or fish stock can be used to thin the soup if necessary.

FROSTED MELON SOUP

Galia or other melons can also be used to make this fresh and pretty soup.

- 1 large cantaloupe melon
- juice of 3 lemons
- 300 ml/½ pint/1 cup water
- 25 g/1 oz sugar
- 100 ml/3 fl oz/⅓ cup dry sherry or white wine
- 150 ml/¼ pint/½ cup whipped cream
- small cube of fresh ginger

Grate the rind from two of the lemons before squeezing the juice from all three.

Cut the melon in half, scoop out and discard the seeds. Scrape out the flesh from the melon and put in a blender goblet. Put the washed and chopped melon skin, lemon juice, sugar and the chopped ginger — there is no need to peel it — in the water and bring to the boil. Cook for 10 or 12 minutes, strain and cool.

When cool, put half the liquid with the melon flesh in the blender and whiz until smooth. There should be about a litre.

Return to a bowl and add the wine. Taste for seasoning and texture — it may not need the balance of the melon water. The cream can either be mixed into the soup, which makes the flavour a little bland, or spooned on top. Serve chilled, in ice-cream glasses or china soup cups, with grated lemon rind and mint leaves scattered over the top.

APPLE AND CIDER SOUP

This unusual soup with a fresh zingy taste can be served hot or cold and garnished as appropriate to the season.

- 4 large cooking apples
- 300 ml/½ pint/1¼ cup Bulmer's Linden Village cider or similar dry cider
- 2 large onions
- 2 cloves garlic
- 2 sprigs each mint and thyme
- pinch each ground cloves and mace
- 2 tablespoons butter
- 600 ml/1 pint/1½ cups vegetable stock
- salt and black pepper

Heat the butter in a large saucepan and add the peeled and finely chopped apples, onions and garlic. Add the spices and herbs and cook until the onions are soft. Pour in the cider and bubble for a few moments, then add two-thirds of the stock, cooking for about 10 minutes more. Purée in a blender or food processor until smooth and return to the saucepan.

Taste for seasoning, adding more spice or sugar if necessary — the flavour should be fruity, spicy and fairly sharp.

Reheat, adding the balance of the stock as required to give a nice consistency, and simmer for a few moments longer. Chill for about 3 hours. The soup is also good served hot.

Serve garnished with spoonfuls of cream or Greek yoghurt, topped with grated lemon peel or chives.

CUCUMBER, SPRING ONION AND MINT SOUP

A fresh, crisp, almost instant soup.

- 2 medium cucumbers
- 8–10 spring onions (scallions)
- 6–8 large mint leaves
- 1 tablespoon chopped parsley
- 1 litre/1¾ pints/5 cups vegetable stock
- 2 or 3 tablespoons Greek yoghurt or fromage frais
- 2 cloves garlic
- 1 tablespoon lemon juice
- Tabasco or chilli powder to taste

Wash and dry the cucumbers, split in two lengthways and scoop out the seeds with a teaspoon. Roughly chop the cucumber and put into a blender goblet. Reserve 2 or 3 scallions for the garnish and add the rest, roughly chopped, with the garlic, mint leaves, parsley and lemon juice to the blender. Add half the stock and purée until smooth, then transfer to a large bowl. Add the balance of the stock, the Greek yoghurt, or fromage frais, and a pinch of salt if required. Chill for about 2 hours to allow the flavours to develop.

Taste for seasoning, adding a dash of Tabasco or chilli powder to taste, and serve garnished with the finely chopped scallions and a few more mint leaves.

GARLIC AND ALMOND SOUP

A creamy and subtle cold soup for garlic lovers.

- 5 cloves garlic
- 100 g/4 oz/¾ cup ground almonds
- 6 slices stale white bread
- 1 litre/1¾ pints/5 cups chicken stock
- 5 tablespoons olive oil
- 3 tablespoons white wine vinegar
- salt and black pepper to taste

Remove the crusts from the bread, soak in water for 10 minutes, then squeeze dry. Peel the garlic and put it with the salt in a mini-processor or use a pestle and mortar.

Mix in the bread and add the oil gradually, as for mayonnaise, then add the vinegar, drop by drop, tasting, and beating well. When a nice creamy mass is formed, gradually thin out with cold water until you get a nice consistency. Check the seasoning, adding more salt or vinegar, or a little oil if it is too salty. Chill for 2 or 3 hours before serving.

White grapes cut in two, with the seeds removed, make an attractive garnish.

SUMMER VEGETABLE SOUPS

TOMATO AND ORANGE SOUP

I don't know who originally thought of this felicitous combination, but it makes one of the most interesting of soups, either hot or cold. The flavour of this version is pungent and spicy — it can be tamed by adding cream. If the only tomatoes to be had are of the pale and watery variety, a discreet amount of tomato purée, say 2–3 teaspoons, can be added, or use canned Italian tomatoes.

- 900 g/2 lb ripe vine tomatoes
- 2 oranges
- 1 large onion, finely chopped
- 1 stick celery, finely chopped
- 2 cloves garlic, chopped
- 1 carrot, grated
- 2 tablespoons olive oil
- 1.2 litres/1¾ pints/5 cups light vegetable stock
- 150 ml/¼ pint/½ cup cream, optional
- 1 sprig thyme
- 1 teaspoon sugar
- cream, see below
- salt and cayenne pepper

Grate the rind of the two oranges, squeeze out the juice and set aside.

Put the onion and garlic in a large saucepan with the olive oil. Cook gently until the onion is softened, then add the celery, carrot and the sprig of thyme, cooking for a few moments longer. Wash the tomatoes and with a sharp knife cut out the core at the stalk end, then roughly chop and add to the saucepan with the orange rind and one pint of the stock. Bring to the boil and simmer gently for 10 minutes. Now remove the thyme and put the soup through a blender — it may be necessary to do this twice to get a smooth texture — and return to the saucepan. Add the orange juice and enough of the remaining stock to give a nice consistency.

Check the seasoning, being careful with the cayenne and adding a pinch more sugar if the tomatoes are very acid. Reheat gently before serving.

If cream is to be added, boil it for a few moments before adding to the hot soup, as the acid in the tomatoes may cause it to curdle.

If the soup is served chilled, it may need to be thinned out with a little cream or stock. It can be garnished with a spoonful of crème fraîche and a paper-thin slice of orange on top.

Caraway rye bread (page 103), cut in very thin slices, is good with this soup.

DILL AND CUCUMBER SOUP

This delicately flavoured soup is quick and easy to make.
Use mint instead of dill for a more summery flavour.

- 2–3 sprigs fresh dill, or ½ teaspoon dried
- 900 g/2 lb cucumber
- 1 large onion, finely chopped
- 1 tablespoon olive oil
- 1 litre/1¾ pints/5 cups milk
- 3 egg yolks
- 150 ml/¼ pint/½ cup cream
- juice of half a lemon
- 2–3 pickled gherkins to garnish, optional
- salt and pepper

Cut the cucumber in half, scrape out the seeds and chop
finely. Heat the oil in a large saucepan, gently cook the
onion until soft, add the cucumber and continue cooking for
5–6 minutes. Add the milk, seasoning and dill and simmer for
a further 10 minutes. Purée in a blender or food processor
and return to the saucepan. Check the seasoning.

Beat the eggs and the cream together thoroughly, pour a
little of the cooled soup on to the eggs, stir well, then
return all to the saucepan. Add lemon juice to taste and
reheat, but don't allow it to boil. If the soup is too thick, it
can be thinned with a little hot milk or cream.

Garnish with the finely chopped gherkins and dill sprigs or
a little fresh salsa (page 79).

COURGETTE AND
CORIANDER SOUP

Courgettes make wonderful patio plants, their trailing habit
and lovely yellow flowers (which can be stuffed and baked,
or deep fried) giving a lush feel to the smallest area.
Coriander does well in pots too.

- 675 g/1½ lb courgettes
- 2–3 tablespoons finely chopped fresh coriander
  or 1 teaspoon ground coriander seeds
- 1 large Spanish onion
- 2 cloves garlic
- 1 small celery stick
- 2 tablespoons butter and 1 tablespoon olive oil
- 1 litre/1¾ pints/5 cups vegetable stock
- salt and black pepper

Chop the onion, celery and garlic finely and put in a
saucepan with the butter and oil. Cook over a gentle heat
until the onion is softened. Chop or grate the unpeeled
courgettes and add to the saucepan with the coriander,
tossing about until the butter is absorbed. Pour in the hot
stock gradually, season well, then cover and simmer until
the courgettes are tender, about 15 minutes.

A few coriander or fennel leaves can be scattered over the
top, or pats of red pepper butter (page 76) for colour.
Courgette bread (page 110) will intensify the flavour.

LOVAGE SOUP

The leaves of this interesting plant make an excellent soup with a sharp celery-lemony flavour redolent of summer. The leaves freeze well if you want to keep some for winter use.

- 5 heaped tablespoons finely chopped lovage leaves
- 2 sticks celery
- 2 onions
- 1 clove garlic
- 2 medium potatoes
- 1 litre/1¾ pints/5 cups chicken or vegetable stock
- 50 g/2 oz/4 tablespoons butter
- 1 tablespoon grated lemon rind
- salt and black pepper
- 3–4 tablespoons crème fraîche
- lemon balm or parsley to garnish

Melt the butter in a large saucepan and sauté the finely chopped onions and celery until soft but not brown, about 15 minutes.

Add the peeled and cubed potatoes and the lovage leaves and continue to cook for a few moments until the butter is absorbed. Add the hot stock, the seasoning and the lemon rind and simmer for 10 minutes or so, until the potato is soft. The soup can be puréed at this point if a smooth soup is preferred. A little more stock can be added if required.

Garnish with the crème fraîche and the chopped lemon balm, or finely chopped parsley.

SOUP SANTÉ

This was a favourite spring soup of the eighteenth century, originally from France, though it became something of a national dish in Ireland. It includes a mixture of fresh green mineral-rich leaves such as spinach, sorrel and watercress, and probably served the same anti-scorbutic purpose as the traditional Irish spring nettle soup. The balance of leaves can be varied according to what is available.

- 175 g/4 oz watercress
- 50 g/2 oz mixed fresh herbs (marjoram, chives etc.)
- 200 g/8 oz spinach
- 50 g/2 oz sorrel
- 2–3 shallots
- 175 g/6 oz/1¼ cups potato, cut in small cubes
- 1 litre/1¾ pints/5 cups light vegetable stock
- 2 egg yolks
- 150 ml/¼ pint/½ cup cream
- finely chopped parsley or herb butter to garnish

Wash the leaves and shake dry, removing any hard stalks from the spinach and sorrel.

Chop roughly. Melt the butter in a large saucepan and gently cook the finely chopped shallots until tender. Add the potatoes, herbs and the chopped leaves to the pan and toss around to absorb the butter, then add the hot stock gradually, stirring well.

Continue cooking gently for about 15 minutes until the potatoes are tender, then purée the soup in a blender or food processor. Return the soup to the saucepan.

Traditionally at this point the soup is thickened further by the addition of the beaten eggs and cream, but I find that this obscures the fresh herby taste of the soup, so if the consistency is thick enough I usually just add the cream. If the eggs are being used, put them with the cream in a small bowl and beat lightly. Add a ladleful of the slightly cooled soup, stir well and return to the saucepan, stirring well. Reheat the soup gently but do not let it boil.

CREAM OF ASPARAGUS SOUP

A classic soup to be enjoyed when asparagus is at its best in early summer. The white asparagus, in season later, is equally delicious.

- ■ 16 spears fresh asparagus
- ■ 175 g/6 oz/1 cup potato
- ■ 2 medium leeks
- ■ 50 g/2 oz/4 tablespoons butter
- ■ 1 litre/1¾ pints/5 cups light chicken stock
- ■ 4 tablespoons crème fraîche
- ■ salt and black pepper

Cut the tips from half the asparagus spears and set aside for garnish. Peel the woody lower parts of the stalks and chop into small pieces. Peel and cube the potatoes. Wash and finely chop the leeks. Blanch the reserved asparagus tips in boiling salted water for 5 minutes, then cool under cold water and set aside.

Melt the butter in a large saucepan and cook the leeks gently for a few minutes, then add the potatoes and the chopped asparagus. Add the stock and simmer for about 20 minutes.

Purée the soup in a food processor or blender and return to the saucepan. Add the crème fraîche and a walnut-size lump of butter and stir well. Garnish with the asparagus tips or slices of red pepper butter (page 76).

LETTUCE AND SORREL SOUP

Sorrel, with its acidic, spinach-like leaves, is so versatile and so hard to find in the supermarket that it is well worth growing. Three or four plants in a deep window-box or in the flower bed will provide enough for sauces and soups all summer, and of course it can be found in the wild all over the country during the summer months.

- 100 g/4 oz sorrel leaves, prepared
- 225 g/8 oz butternut type lettuce
- 2 shallots
- 2 cloves garlic
- 175 g/6 oz/1¼ cups peas
- 2 medium potatoes
- 50 g/2 oz/4 tablespoons butter
- 2 tablespoons finely chopped fresh marjoram
- 1 litre/1¾ pints/5 cups light vegetable stock
- 4–5 tablespoons cream
- 1 rounded tablespoon flour
- 2 tablespoons chives to garnish
- fleurons (page 84), optional
- salt and black pepper

Wash the sorrel, shake dry and cut away the centre ribs and any damaged pieces. Wash and shake dry the lettuce and cut it, with the sorrel, into fine strips. Melt the butter in a large saucepan and add the very finely chopped potato, marjoram, garlic, peas, shallot, lettuce and sorrel. Cook gently until the potato is almost tender and the sorrel and lettuce almost melted. Sprinkle in the flour and stir well until it is cooked, 2 or 3 minutes, then gradually add the hot stock, stirring until the soup has thickened slightly. Continue cooking for a further 3 or 4 minutes.

Check the seasoning, then purée the soup in a blender, or use a hand-held blender, and return it to the saucepan. Add the cream and reheat gently. Garnish this lovely buttery soup with fleurons (page 84) and sprinkle with the chives.

SPINACH AND BLUE CHEESE SOUP

- 450 g/1 lb fresh spinach
- 75 g/3 oz/6 tablespoons Cashel Blue or Roquefort cheese
- 75 g/3 oz/6 tablespoons butter
- 1 litre/1¾ pints/5 cups chicken stock
- 300 ml/½ pint/1 cup cream
- 1 tablespoon flour
- blue cheese butter (page 77)
- salt and pepper

Wash the spinach and shake dry, removing any dead leaves or hard stems. Melt the butter in a large saucepan and add the spinach, cooking for 5 or 6 minutes until the spinach has wilted.

If you are using frozen spinach, defrost and squeeze out as much water as possible, then add to the butter in the pan. Add the flour and cook, stirring, for 2 or 3 minutes. Stir in the hot stock and the cream gradually and continue cooking for a few minutes. Purée the soup in a food processor or blender. Return to the saucepan and add the finely chopped or crumbled cheese, stirring well until the cheese has melted. Reheat gently and serve hot with pats of blue cheese butter floating on top.

WINTER VEGETABLE SOUPS

CARROT AND ORANGE SOUP

A soup with a vibrant colour and fresh flavour, good when fresh green vegetables are in short supply.

- 900 g/1½ lb carrots
- 2 oranges
- 1 onion
- 1 stick celery
- 1 litre/1¾ pints/5 cups light vegetable stock
- 1 medium potato
- 50 g/2 oz/4 tablespoons butter
- ½ teaspoon Chinese five spice powder or caraway seeds
- salt and black pepper

Grate the rind of the oranges, squeeze out the juice and set aside. Finely chop the carrots, celery, onion and potato. Melt the butter in a large saucepan and gently cook the onion until soft, but don't let it brown. Add the other vegetables and the orange rind and stir for a few minutes to absorb the butter before adding the stock. Cook gently until the vegetables are soft then purée or blend thoroughly.

Return to the saucepan and season with salt and black pepper. Add the five spice powder, a pinch at a time, until it is to your taste — if it's a freshly opened container the flavour can be quite powerful. Just before serving add the orange juice and reheat gently.

The soup can be garnished with spoonfuls of whipped cream or mascarpone softened with a spoonful of orange or lime juice, and very thin slices of orange.

FENNEL AND POTATO SOUP

A smooth white soup with the delicate faintly aniseed flavour of fennel.

- 2 large bulbs fennel
- 3 medium potatoes, peeled and quartered
- 1 large onion
- 3 cloves garlic
- 2 tablespoons butter
- 2 tablespoons olive oil
- 1 litre/1¾ pints/5 cups vegetable stock
- 150 ml/¼ pint/½ cup white wine
- ½ teaspoon each cayenne and five spice powder
- salt to taste

Cut the fennel bulbs in two and set aside any feathery green fronds for the garnish. Cut out the hard cores and remove any damaged outer leaves, then cut into thin slices.

Place the fennel, onion, potatoes, garlic and spices in a large saucepan with the butter and oil. Sauté for 6 or 7 minutes, then add a ladleful of the stock and the white wine, cover and cook very gently until the fennel is soft. Add the rest of the stock, check the seasoning, and simmer for a few moments more.

Purée in a blender or food processor until smooth, taste for seasoning, and serve with green fennel fronds on top.

TURNIP AND YELLOW PEPPER SOUP

The homely turnip is transformed by the smoky flavour of the pepper in this lovely golden soup.

- 225 g/8 oz turnip, peeled and cubed
- 2 large yellow peppers, cubed
- 1 onion, finely chopped
- 1 litre/1¾ pints/5 cups chicken or vegetable stock
- ½ teaspoon each ground cumin and nutmeg
- 2 teaspoons paprika
- 1 tablespoon olive oil
- 1 tablespoon butter
- salt and black pepper

Remove the seeds and pith from the peppers and chop into cubes. In a large saucepan gently sauté the peppers and onion in the oil and butter until soft, but not browned. Add the spices and stir about for a few moments. Now add the turnip and three-quarters of the stock and simmer until the vegetables are tender. Purée the soup in a blender until smooth, add salt and black pepper to taste, and dilute with the reserved stock, reheat and serve.

If a more textured soup is preferred, just purée one cupful of the soup, return it to the saucepan, reheat and serve.

A few slices of streaky bacon, chopped and crisply fried in butter, make an excellent garnish.

LEEK AND POTATO SOUP

Leeks are one of the oldest of our pot vegetables. They found a natural partner when the potato arrived in Ireland in the sixteenth century. Recipes for leek and potato soups abound and there are no hard and fast rules. The quantity of leek to potato can be adjusted to your taste.

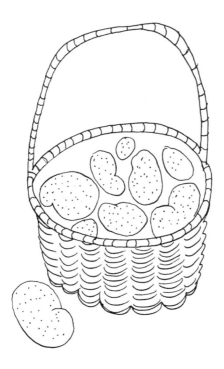

- 575 g/1¼ lb leeks
- 3 medium potatoes
- 3 sticks celery
- 2 large cloves garlic
- 50 g/2 oz/4 tablespoons butter
- 1.2 litres/2 pints/5½ cups light chicken or vegetable stock
- salt and pepper
- 3 scallions, very finely chopped
- 2 tablespoons chopped chervil or parsley
- potato croûtons (page 81)

Peel and chop the potatoes into cubes. Finely chop the garlic, the cleaned leeks and the celery. Melt the butter in a large saucepan, add the vegetables and gently cook for about 10 minutes or so until the butter is absorbed, but don't allow to brown. Add three-quarters of the stock and simmer until the potatoes are soft, about 15 minutes. Purée the soup in two batches in a blender and add the balance of the stock.

Soups with a large proportion of potato tend to thicken if left to stand for any length of time. They can be thinned with more stock or milk.

To serve, mix the croûtons, scallions and parsley together and mound a large spoonful on top of each bowl.

CREAM OF CELERY SOUP

- 675 g/1½ lb prepared celery
- 2 small potatoes
- 1 large onion
- 4 tablespoons butter
- 900 ml/1½ pints/4½ cups vegetable stock
- 1 tablespoon chopped lovage or fennel leaves or 1 teaspoon celery or fennel seeds
- 1 glass Amontillado sherry
- 2 egg yolks
- 150 ml/¼ pint/½ cup cream
- 2 tablespoons chopped celery leaves
- curry powder
- salt and white pepper

Remove any damaged parts from the celery, keep aside a few leaves for the garnish, wash and dry carefully. Chop the celery, onions and potatoes finely.

Melt the butter in a large saucepan, add the onions and cook gently until soft, then add the potatoes, celery and herbs, tossing around until the butter is absorbed. Add the hot stock and simmer until the celery is tender. Purée in a blender or food processor until completely smooth, then return to the saucepan. Check the seasoning and add a teaspoon or so of curry powder and the glass of sherry. Boil hard for 2 or 3 minutes to cook off the alcohol and concentrate the flavour, then cool the soup slightly. If the soup is too thick, add a very little stock or water.

Beat the eggs with the cream in a bowl and pour in two ladlefuls of the cooled soup, stirring well. Return the mixture to the saucepan, reheat gently and stir until it thickens slightly, but don't let it boil. Garnish with the finely chopped celery leaves.

PALESTINE SOUP

The Jerusalem artichoke, which actually came to Europe from Canada in the seventeenth century, is thought to have got its curious name from the Italian for sunflower, *girasole*, which is a species of the same plant. Wherever it comes from, it makes excellent soup.

- 450 g/1 lb Jerusalem artichokes
- 175 g/6 oz slice cooked ham, finely chopped
- 4 tablespoons butter
- 1 large potato
- 1 litre/1¾ pints/5 cups vegetable stock
- 150 ml/5 oz/½ cup double cream
- ½ teaspoon ground cumin
- 1 tablespoon lemon juice or vinegar
- salt and black pepper
- 4–5 slices hot buttered toast

Scrub the artichokes carefully, then peel and drop into cold water to which a little lemon juice or vinegar has been added.

Melt the butter in a large saucepan and gently cook the onions until transparent. Chop the potato into cubes and add to the saucepan. Dry the artichokes, slice finely and add to the onions and potatoes, stirring well until all the butter is absorbed.

Gradually add the hot stock, half the finely chopped ham, the cumin and seasoning to taste. Cover and cook gently for about 15 to 20 minutes until the vegetables are tender. Purée in a blender or food processor and return to the pan. Check the seasoning, adding a dash of lemon juice if necessary. Add a little stock or milk if the soup is too thick when reheated.

Remove the crusts from the slices of hot toast, butter well and press the remaining chopped ham on top, then cut into little triangles. Float 2 or 3 on top of each bowl of soup.

FRENCH ONION SOUP

This French classic soup is so well known it has been absorbed into the cuisine of many countries. It is given an Irish twist here with the addition of Irish whiskey instead of cognac.

- 450 g/1 lb/4 cups onions
- 12 slices good French bread
- 50 g/2 oz/½ cup grated gruyère cheese
- 25 g/1 oz/¼ cup grated Parmesan cheese
- 50 g/2 oz/4 tablespoons flour
- 15 g/1 oz/2 tablespoons butter
- 2 tablespoons olive oil
- 1.2 litres/2 pints/5¼ cups chicken stock
- 1 glass white wine
- 1 small glass Irish whiskey
- 1 teaspoon sugar
- salt and black pepper
- 4–6 croûtes (page 80)

Heat the oil in a large saucepan and add the onions. Cook very gently until the onions are completely soft, then add the sugar. Stir until dissolved, then increase the heat slightly and cook until the onions are a rich gold colour, perhaps 20 minutes, but don't let them burn.

Add the whiskey to the pan and, standing well back, ignite it with a match. Allow the whiskey to burn for a moment to caramelise the onions, then immediately cover with a lid.

Put in the butter and when it melts add the flour, stirring well for 2 or 3 minutes to cook the flour, then add the wine and hot stock, stirring continually until smooth, scraping up all the brown buttery residues from the bottom of the pan. Add salt and pepper to taste and simmer gently for about 15 or 20 minutes.

Mix the cheeses together, press on to the croûtes, put them in the bottom of heatproof bowls and pour the hot soup over them. When they rise to the surface, add a little more cheese and brown under the grill or in a hot oven.

The soup can be finished in a heatproof tureen if preferred.

ORANGE AND PARSNIP SOUP

The subtle flavour and natural creaminess of parsnips is complemented by the tangy orange in this recipe.

- 1 large orange
- 4 large parsnips
- 50 g/2 oz/4 tablespoons butter
- 1 large Spanish onion
- 1 litre/1¾ pints/5 cups light vegetable stock
- 150 ml/¼ pint/½ cup cream
- ½ teaspoon coriander seeds
- salt and black pepper

Melt the butter in a large saucepan and gently cook the finely chopped onion until soft. Peel and chop the parsnips and add to the onion, stirring around until the butter is absorbed. Add the coriander seeds. Grate the peel of the orange and add to the saucepan. Squeeze the juice and set aside. Add the stock and seasoning and cook gently until the parsnips are soft, then purée in a blender or food processor.

Just before serving, reheat the soup gently, check the seasoning, add the orange juice, simmer for a few moments, then add the cream and reheat gently but don't allow it to boil.

This soup thickens a little if left overnight and can be thinned with a little milk or stock.

BEETROOT CONSOMMÉ WITH SOUR CREAM OR MASCARPONE

Pickled beetroot is so popular in Ireland it is surprising that there are so few indigenous recipes using fresh beetroot, particularly as it grows so well here.

- 450 g/1 1b cooked beetroot (not pickled)
- 2.1 litres/2 pints/5½ cups good chicken stock
- 1 clove garlic
- pinch ground cloves
- 1 small glass dry sherry
- Tabasco
- sour cream or Mascarpone
- half a juicy lemon
- salt

Crush and finely chop the garlic. Put it in a blender with the chopped beetroot and a cupful of the stock and blend until completely smooth. Return to a large saucepan and add the cloves, Tabasco, lemon juice and salt, tasting as you add until the flavour is to your taste. It may need a pinch of sugar. Add the sherry, bring to a gentle simmer for about 10 minutes and serve with sour cream or Mascarpone softened with a dash of lemon juice.

If a clear consommé is more to your taste, separate two eggs and put the yolks aside for another use. Put the egg whites in a small bowl, crush the shells and add them to the whites. Beat well with a fork for a few moments, then beat the mixture into the soup and leave to simmer undisturbed for about 10 minutes.

Have ready a nylon sieve lined with muslin or an old linen tea towel and a bowl large enough to take the soup. When the egg whites and shells have formed a thick crust on top of the soup, very gently pour the lot into the sieve. Allow the soup to drip slowly through into the bowl, resisting the temptation to shake the sieve or otherwise hurry it up. It will take about half an hour or more to drip through and of course the volume will be reduced. There should be sufficient for six small soup cups, which will be enough when the garnish is added.

To make jellied consommé use one packet of gelatine, or three leaves, to each pint of the soup, following the directions on the packet. Jellied consommés look pretty in the saucer type of champagne glass. Garnish as the hot soup.

SPICY SOUPS

SPICY PICKLED CUCUMBER SOUP

Both fresh and pickled cucumbers are combined in an interesting soup with sharp and spicy flavours.

There is quite a variation between different brands of pickled cucumber or gherkins. The Polish or German brands tend to be larger, milder and generally nicer. The Polish brand Krakus is my first choice.

- 1 700 g approx. jar pickled cucumbers
- 1 medium fresh cucumber
- 2 red chillies

- 2 cloves garlic
- 1 litre/1¾ pints/5 cups light vegetable stock
- 1 tablespoon oil
- fresh dill
- sour cream

Cut the washed and unpeeled cucumber in half lengthways and scoop out the seeds. Cut into small cubes and reserve three tablespoons for the garnish.

Peel and very finely chop the garlic. Split the chillies and scrape out the seeds and white pith and cut into fine shreds. Heat the oil in a large saucepan and gently cook the chilli and garlic, being careful not to let the garlic brown. Put in the finely cubed fresh cucumber and three-quarters of the stock and simmer until the cucumber is cooked, about 10 minutes.

Put the pickled cucumber into the blender with the remaining stock and blend until smooth, then add to the saucepan, stirring and cooking for a few minutes more. Serve hot garnished with spoonfuls of sour cream and finely chopped fresh dill or chives and the reserved fresh cucumber sprinkled over the top.

CELERIAC AND GINGER SOUP

The turnip-like appearance of this dull looking root gives no indication of the delicate celery-like flavour within. Choose as large and smooth a celeriac as you can find.

- 570–675 g/1¼–1½ lb celeriac
- 1½ inch piece fresh ginger
- 1 litre/1¾ pints/5 cups chicken stock
- 2 cloves garlic
- 1 strip orange peel
- 1 large onion, finely chopped
- 1 large potato, peeled and cubed
- 1 tablespoon olive oil
- 25 g/1 oz/2 tablespoons butter
- ½ teaspoon ground coriander
- Tabasco or chilli powder
- salt and black pepper
- spicy croûtons (page 81)

Peel the celeriac and potato and cut into small cubes. Melt the butter in a large saucepan and add the oil. Put in the finely chopped onion and cook gently until softened, then add the orange peel, celeriac, coriander and the potato. Grate the washed ginger on a fine grater — there is no need to peel it — and add to the saucepan. Pour in three-quarters of the hot stock and cook until the celeriac is tender, about 20 minutes, then remove the orange peel. Purée the soup and return to the saucepan.

Check the seasoning (it may need more salt) and add Tabasco to taste. Pour in the cream and sufficient of the remaining stock to give a nice consistency, reheat gently and serve garnished with spicy croûtons.

CHICKEN SOUP WITH CHILLIES AND POACHED EGG

This is the perfect soup for the weary and fragile. The restorative ingredients are easy to digest and it is quick to make, especially if there is some chicken stock in the freezer.

- 1 litre/1¾ pints/5 cups strong chicken stock
- 2–3 chillies
- ½ leek
- 1 poached egg per person
- 2–3 slices toasted French roll per person
- 1 clove garlic
- 2–3 tablespoons grated cheese
- salt and black pepper

Put the stock in a large saucepan and add the crushed clove of garlic. Split the chillies in half lengthways, remove the seeds and white pith and with a sharp knife cut into very fine threads. Cut the leek across into three pieces, then split lengthways, slice into thin slivers and add with the chilli to the stock. Simmer gently for 15 minutes or so while you poach the eggs and toast the bread, then test the soup for seasoning and remove the garlic clove.

To serve, put 2 or 3 pieces of bread in each soup plate, place a poached egg on top and pour the soup over the eggs. A little finely grated mature Cheddar or Parmesan can be sprinkled over the top.

To poach the eggs put about 3 inches of boiling water in a wide saucepan or deep frying pan and bring the water back to the boil. Lift the pan off the heat and gently crack each egg into the water, as near to the surface as possible, letting the egg just slide into the water. Cover and leave for 4 to 5 minutes when there should be a white veil over the yolks. Lift out the eggs gently with a slotted spoon, transfer to a warm plate, trimming off any ragged edges, and use immediately.

Poach the eggs 3 at a time, bringing the water back to the boil before cooking the next lot.

ROASTED ONION SOUP

A richly coloured autumnal soup with an interesting smoky flavour, nicely complemented by the black olive paste.

- 775 g/1½ lb red onions
- 4–5 cloves garlic, peeled

- 2 large red peppers
- 450 g/1 lb vine tomatoes
- 200 ml/7 fl oz/1 cup red wine
- 3 tablespoons olive oil
- 2 sprigs each thyme and rosemary
- 1 litre/1¾ pints/5 cups chicken stock
- bouquet garni
- ½ teaspoon chilli powder
- salt and black pepper
- croûtes and black olive paste (tapenade) to garnish

Peel the onions and cut into quarters. Cut the peppers in two and remove the seeds and white pith. Cut the tomatoes in two and place them, with the peppers, cut side up in an ovenproof casserole. Arrange the herbs and garlic between the onions and tomatoes. Dribble the olive oil over the vegetables and roast for 30 minutes at 200°C/400°F/Gas 6 until soft.

Remove the vegetables to a blender or food processor, discarding the herbs. Add a little of the stock and purée the vegetables thoroughly until smooth. This will have to be done in two batches. Pour the vegetable purée into a large saucepan, add the wine and the remainder of the stock, season well and simmer gently for about 15 minutes.

If a smoother soup is preferred, push the soup through a sieve and return to the saucepan to reheat.

Place a croûte (page 80) spread with black olive paste in each bowl and pour the soup over them.

AUBERGINE AND RED PEPPER SOUP

An interesting soup with an intense, slightly smoky flavour.

- 1 large aubergine
- 2 large red peppers
- 275 g/½ lb/2 cups red onions
- 1 sprig thyme
- ½ red chilli/½ teaspoon five spice powder
- 2 teaspoons paprika
- 1 litre/1¾ pints/5 cups vegetable stock
- 2 tablespoons olive oil
- crème fraîche
- 3–4 scallions, finely chopped, to garnish

Heat the oven to 220°C/425°F/Gas 7. Put the aubergine and the peppers on a baking tray and bake for about 40 minutes, until the aubergine is soft. Remove from the oven and cover with a tea towel until cool enough to handle.

Meanwhile, heat the olive oil in a large saucepan and gently sweat the onions until soft. Remove the seeds and pith from the chilli, chop finely and add to the onions. Cut the cooled aubergine in half and with a spoon scrape out the flesh, adding it to the pan. Cut the peppers in half, saving as much of the juice as possible, and peel off the skin, discarding it with the pith and seeds. Add the flesh to the saucepan with the spices, herbs and three-quarters of the stock. Cook gently for 20 minutes, then purée until smooth.

Return to the saucepan, add the balance of the stock if required, reheat and serve. Garnish with spoonfuls of crème fraîche topped with the finely chopped scallions.

Garnishes

Flavoured Butters

Use flavoured butters for a final flourish to soups; they have a slightly thickening effect and give a fresh flavour lift. Choose a butter either to enhance the soup flavour or contrast with it. The basil butter recipe can be adapted using other herbs such as sun-dried tomatoes.

RED PEPPER BUTTER

This intensely flavoured butter is enhanced by the aromatic spiciness of the paprika.

- 50 g/2 oz/4 tablespoons finely chopped red pepper
- 2 teaspoons paprika
- 100 g/4 oz/8 tablespoons butter
- 1 extra tablespoon butter
- salt

Melt the tablespoon of butter in a small saucepan and gently cook the red pepper and paprika together until the pepper is soft. Push the pepper mixture through a sieve and mash thoroughly into the butter. A mini-blender is ideal for this purpose.

Shape into a roll, wrap in clingfilm and store in the fridge for a few days, or the freezer for longer storage.

BLUE CHEESE BUTTER

- 50 g/2 oz/4 tablespoons Cashel Blue or Roquefort cheese
- 75 g/3 oz/6 tablespoons butter
- freshly ground black pepper
- 2 teaspoons lemon juice

Mash the cheese thoroughly, then work into the softened butter. Add 1 or 2 grinds of pepper and the lemon juice, shape into a roll and wrap in clingfilm. Store in the fridge until required, or freeze for longer storage.

BASIL BUTTER

- 20 g/¾ oz fresh basil leaves
- 100 g/4 oz/8 tablespoons butter
- salt and black pepper
- 2 teaspoons lemon juice

Wash and dry the basil and remove the stalks. Chop very finely and mash into the softened butter with one or two grinds of pepper, salt and lemon juice to taste. Form into a roll and wrap in clingfilm. Store in the fridge for a few days, or the freezer for longer storage.

ANCHOVY BUTTER

- 50 g/2 oz tin/¼ cup anchovies
- 100 g/4 oz/8 tablespoons butter
- black pepper
- 2 teaspoons lemon juice

Pour the oil off the anchovies and mash well with the lemon juice and black pepper. Work the mixture into the softened butter, then shape into a roll 1½ inches in diameter, wrap in clingfilm and store in the fridge or freezer until required.

SUN-DRIED TOMATO BUTTER

- 100 g/4 oz/8 tablespoons butter
- 3 sun-dried tomatoes, packed in oil
- 1 teaspoon lemon juice
- salt and black pepper

Work the tomatoes, butter and lemon juice together in a mini-blender and season with salt and black pepper, shape into a 1½ inch roll and store in the fridge or freezer until required.

HERB BUTTER

- 3–4 tablespoons mixed fresh herbs (mint, parsley, coriander, rocket etc.), finely chopped
- very little sage, thyme or rosemary
- 100 g/4 oz/8 tablespoons butter
- black pepper

Mash the herbs into the butter with a few grinds of black pepper. Shape into a roll, wrap in clingfilm and store in the fridge for a few days, or the freezer for longer storage.

FRESH SALSA

- 2 tablespoons red pepper
- 1 tablespoon green pepper
- 1 tablespoon scallions
- 1 tablespoon capers
- 1 tablespoon coriander and parsley
- 1–2 tablespoons olive oil
- lemon juice to taste

Very finely chop the ingredients. Give half the quantity a brief whiz in a mini-processor, then mix all together. Add a pinch of salt, the olive oil and lemon juice to taste. Salsas give an instant lift of colour and flavour to creamy mild soups.

Put tiny spoonfuls on top of cream or crème fraîche garnishes, or float directly on top of the soup.

Croûtes

CROÛTES

Cut slices of baguette or French roll diagonally into thin slices and dry in a cool oven until crisp but not browned. Croûtes and croûtons can be flavoured with spices or cheese.

CHEESE CROÛTES

Spread the dried croûtes with a little grated mature Cheddar, gruyère or Parmesan and return to the oven for a few minutes, or brown under the grill. Place in the bottom of soup plates, or a tureen, and pour the hot soup over them.

CROÛTONS

Cut the crusts off 3 or 4 pieces of sliced bread. Cut lengthways into thin fingers, then cut across into small cubes. Fry the cubes in a mixture of olive oil and butter until crisp. Drain on kitchen paper.

SPICY CROÛTONS

Toss the freshly made croûtons in a mixture of curry powder, paprika and a little nutmeg, or spices of your choice.

POTATO CROÛTONS

- 3 medium potatoes
- 1 or 2 teaspoons paprika
- oil for frying

Peel the potatoes, cut into cubes and immerse in cold water for about 20 minutes. Drain and dry thoroughly in a tea towel, then sprinkle with the paprika, or cayenne for a hotter flavour. Heat 3 or 4 tablespoons of oil in a frying pan over a moderate heat and fry the potatoes until tender, nicely browned and crisp. Drain on kitchen paper and sprinkle with salt just before serving.

Dumplings

EGG BALLS

- 3 eggs
- 1 tablespoon breadcrumbs
- salt and black pepper
- 1 teaspoon very finely chopped chives
- salt to taste

Hard boil two of the eggs, cool, then rub them through a sieve. Add the yolk from the remaining egg, the breadcrumbs and the seasoning. Flour your hands and roll the mixture into tiny balls. Drop into the boiling soup and simmer for 5–10 minutes. They can also be cooked in boiling salted water and added to the soup before serving.

CHICKEN DUMPLINGS

- 100 g/4 oz/1 small skinless chicken breast
- 50 g/2 oz breadcrumbs
- ½ teaspoon grated lemon rind
- 1 small egg
- pinch thyme or sage
- salt and black pepper

Remove any trace of skin or fat from the chicken breast and either mince or, using a sharp chopping knife, chop the chicken very finely, almost to a paste. This is almost as fast as using a food processor and gives a lighter texture to the dumplings. Season the chicken with the salt, black pepper, lemon rind and herbs.

Rub the chicken into the breadcrumbs, then using about half the beaten egg, mix lightly until the mixture sticks together. Form into small dumplings with a teaspoon. Roll them in flour and poach for 5–6 minutes in 300 ml (½ pint) of stock or simmering salted water. This quantity will make 18 marble-sized dumplings.

SAUSAGE DUMPLINGS

- 225 g/8 oz pure pork sausages or sausage meat
- 4 tablespoons day-old bread crumbs
- pinch dried mixed herbs

If using sausages, remove the skins and mix all the ingredients well together, then with floured hands form into marble-sized balls and drop into stock or boiling water until cooked, about 15 minutes. If necessary, a very few drops of milk can be added to bind the mixture together.

Excellent in pea soup and good with lentil and bean soups too.

FLUFFY DUMPLINGS

- 75 g/3 oz/¾ cup self-raising flour
- 75 g/3 oz/¾ cup white breadcrumbs
- 38 g/1½ oz/3 tablespoons butter
- 2 beaten eggs
- cayenne to taste

Put the flour, breadcrumbs, seasoning and herbs into a bowl and rub in the butter with your fingers. Add sufficient beaten egg to make a dough just stiff enough to hold together. Scoop up small quantities with a dessertspoon and, with floured hands, form into small balls about the size of a walnut shell, and cook in gently simmering soup or salted water for about 20 minutes. This quantity makes about 20 dumplings. Allow about 3 or 4 per serving.

Pastry Garnishes

FLEURONS

Roll out puff pastry ¼ inch thick, or use ready rolled. Cut into stars, crescents or preferred shape and bake until golden brown. The pastry can also be brushed with beaten egg and strewn with seeds or coarse salt.

CHEESE STRAWS

- 75 g/3 oz/6 tablespoons mixed mature Cheddar and Parmesan
- 100 g/¼ lb/1 cup plain flour
- 50 g/2 oz/4 tablespoons butter
- 2 egg yolks
- ¼ teaspoon cayenne or chilli powder
- small pinch salt
- 1 tablespoon poppy seeds, optional

Rub the softened butter into the flour and salt, add the cayenne and the cheese and combine into a paste with the egg yolks. Form into a long strip ¼ inch thick and four inches wide, dampen slightly with a few drops of milk, then sprinkle with poppy seeds. Cut the dough across into ½ inch wide strips then, holding the strips at each end and twisting in opposite directions, lay them on a baking sheet lined with baking paper.

Bake for about 10–12 minutes at 200°C/400°F/Gas 6 until just golden brown, taking care they don't get too brown.

Makes about 25.

SESAME BISCUITS

These delicious biscuits are very good with light chilled soups where bread is perhaps a little too heavy. Cumin or caraway seeds can be used also.

- 1 tablespoon sesame seeds
- 200 g/6 oz/1½ cups plain flour
- 125 g/4½ oz/9 tablespoons butter, chilled
- 25 g/1 oz/2 tablespoons grated Parmesan
- 1 egg yolk
- ¼ teaspoon chilli powder
- pinch salt

Put the flour into a bowl with a pinch of salt and the chilli powder. Cut the butter into small cubes and rub into the flour until it looks like coarse breadcrumbs.

Add the Parmesan and sesame seeds, mixing with a fork. Beat the egg yolks together with a fork and stir into the flour mixture, then mixing with your hands, as lightly as possible, draw in all the flour and knead lightly to form a cylinder about 4 cm (1½ inches) in diameter. If the dough is too dry, add a teaspoon or so of water.

With a sharp knife cut the roll into slices about ¾ cm (¼ inch) thick, place on a baking tray lined with silicone baking paper and bake at 180°C/350°F/Gas 4 for 12 minutes. The biscuits are very crumbly when hot, so leave until cold before handling gently.

Made a little smaller, these biscuits are excellent served with drinks.

Breads

Introduction

Ireland is unusual among European countries today in that many of the traditional breads such as wholemeal, white soda and currant bread, using bread soda or baking powder, are still made daily in many homes across the country.

Baking soda, however, was not in general use until the nineteenth century, and in earlier times the breads made in the simpler farm homes were barley and oat flat breads. The most widespread method of baking for centuries was over the open fire, but the wall oven, located at the side of the open fireplace, was often a feature of comfortable farm homes from quite early times.

In the past wheat bread was also made extensively in the home using the yeasty froth, or barm, produced when brewing ale or beer. However, with the decline of home brewing, as beer and ale gradually became factory products or lost favour to tea and coffee, yeast-leavened bread became the province of the town baker, his bread even reaching into the countryside.

The Hallowe'en bread, barm breac, or brack, an enriched and yeast-leavened bread dough with dried fruit, spices and eggs, and originally coloured with saffron, is the exception and continued to be made at home.

In recent years there has been a great revival of interest in yeast-raised breads, reflected in the number of leading chefs turning their attention to ever more interesting and inventive breads, flavoured and shaped to complement their particular cuisine.

This interest is timely as it has never been easier to make yeast bread. The aura of difficulty and uncertainty connected with yeast, probably folk memories from the days of ale barm, has been dispelled. Dried yeast, predictable and easy to use, is available everywhere. If, in addition, there is a food processor or mixer with a dough hook, the bread practically makes itself, and if kneading dough by hand is necessary, it is in fact rather a pleasurable task and takes only a few minutes.

Yeasts

Instant dried yeasts with 'improvers', additives that help the dough to rise quickly and similar to those used in commercial baking, can be found in most supermarkets. Instant dried yeast, using only ascorbic acid (vitamin C) as an accelerator, and also traditional dried yeast, can be found in most health or wholefood stores. The directions for both types will be found on the packets. The instant form is simply mixed in with the flour and salt; the traditional form is mixed to a cream with a little warm water and a teaspoon of sugar and allowed to froth before mixing in with the flour. The brand I prefer to use is Allinson's, which is available in both instant and traditional forms, and is available in health and wholefood shops.

Fresh yeast is not as readily available as dried yeast, but when a source is found it can safely be bought in quantity as it freezes well. A half-ounce/12 g/½ tablespoon is sufficient for 675g/1½ lb of flour.

Remember that cold will inhibit the development of yeast, but it won't kill it. Heat however will, so be sure to use only hand-hot liquid when mixing your dough.

Bread does take time to rise, but once it is prepared and left to rise, which takes about 10 minutes, it needn't be your time. Dough left to rise for an hour and a half can safely be left for 3 or 4 hours if necessary, particularly whole-wheat or rye doughs which benefit from slow rising. And if it's prepared at night, it can be safely left alone in a cool room until the morning, the air knocked out of it, and left again until the evening, kneading it for a moment before baking.

Why would you want to make your own bread? Well, it's fun and very satisfying to see and eat the finished product. And then there are considerations such as flavour, texture, variety and purity; depending on the flour and yeast you choose, it can be made without additives. Also, there is no end to the shapes, mixtures and flavours you can play with — all good reasons to give it a try.

Flour

The flour most suitable for making basic white bread is strong white wheat flour. Wheat contains proteins that form gluten when dough is made. When gluten develops in the dough, it forms a substance that traps the tiny gas-filled bubbles produced by wheat activity and which aerate the dough, making the bread light. 'Hard' or 'strong' wheats have a gluten content of 12–15 per cent which allows the dough to hold more water and to expand more, thus producing a greater volume than 'soft' wheat flours, which have a lower gluten content, say, 8–10 per cent.

In Ireland very little hard wheat is grown, our climate being more favourable to soft wheat, which has a good flavour and is used for general baking and cake-making. Such flour is sold as plain or household white flour.

For commercial bread-making, our own soft wheat is blended with imported hard wheats, and it is a mixture of this type which is sold as strong white flour. Until recently most white flour was bleached to make it more attractive in appearance, but this practice has been discontinued.

American all-purpose flour is somewhat similar to our strong flour and can be used for both bread and cakes, and American Graham flours are similar to our wheatmeal or wholewheat flours.

Wheatmeal flours vary in wholemeal and bran content, from 100 per cent to about 75 per cent depending on the brand, and a little experimentation will allow the choice of a flour that suits your taste. Wheatmeal flours are usually a mixture of soft and hard wheats.

Wholemeal flours are, of course, whole meal. The thing to look for here is 'stone ground', which is considered to leave more of the natural nutrients in the flour than flour ground with steel rollers.

Rye, barley, oatmeal and maize flours lack that superior wheat-type gluten, so to make a light bread they need a proportion of wheat flour — in the past these grains were usually prepared as flat breads, to be eaten as soon as they were cooked.

The term 'meal' usually refers to coarsely ground flours; the term 'flour' is used to describe the finely ground grades.

Many of the following recipes are adapted from old manuscripts and cookery books which reflect the changing fortunes of various grains; others are adaptations of the numerous breads which have been absorbed into our national cuisine in recent years, and reflect the worldwide internationalisation of food.

Most of the recipes can be made in half quantities for purposes of experiment, but when doubling recipes it is not necessary to double the quantity of yeast — just add an extra 50 per cent.

YEAST BREADS

HERB BREAD

The pronounced but subtle herb flavour in this bread is due in part to the fresh sage. If dried sage or thyme have to be used, a quarter-teaspoon of each will be enough. Try this bread with mild and creamy soups or use it to make crostini, bruschetta or toasted croûtes. To vary the flavour other herbs can be used instead.

- 450 g/1 lb/4 cups plain flour
- 300 g/½ pint/1¼ cups warm milk and water
- 1 tablespoon or 1 sachet instant yeast
- 1 teaspoon salt
- 8–10 fresh sage leaves
- 1 sprig fresh thyme
- ½ tablespoon fennel seeds
- 1 teaspoon sugar

Wash and dry the sage leaves and chop finely. Crush the seeds slightly. Measure the flour into a large bowl and mix in the salt, fennel seeds, sage, sugar and yeast, or follow directions on the packet, using water from the measured quantity. Make a well in the centre of the flour, pour in the water and milk mixture and knead well, drawing in the dry flour gradually until a silky dough is achieved. This takes about 2 minutes in a mixer with a dough hook, or 3 or 4 minutes by hand on a floured surface.

Wipe out the bowl and oil it with a piece of kitchen paper and a teaspoon of oil. Return the dough to the oiled bowl, cover loosely with clingfilm or a tea towel and set in a warm place until the dough doubles in bulk, about an hour.

Knock the air out of the dough and knead for a moment or two in the bowl, or stretch and pull the dough by hand on a floured surface. Shape the dough into a high round ball, tucking the edges underneath, and place on a floured baking sheet. With a very sharp knife make 3 shallow incisions across the top of the ball, about an inch apart, then do the same in the opposite direction. Brush over with a spoonful of cream, or beaten egg, leave for a further 20 minutes or so to recover volume. Bake at 230°C/450°F/Gas 8 for 15 minutes, then reduce the heat to 200°C/400°F/Gas 6 for a further 20 minutes. The bread is cooked when it gives a hollow sound when tapped underneath.

BREAKFAST ROLLS

This is a very old recipe, from the 1760s, and gives a roll with a slightly soft crust and lovely creamy crumb which keeps fresh for 2 or 3 days. It can be reheated successfully and toasts very well.

This type of roll was eaten for breakfast and dinner by the fashionable classes in the eighteenth century, when coffee and tea began to take the place of ale caudles, possets and broths at breakfast time.

- 675 g/1½ lb/6 cups plain white flour
- 3 large eggs
- 4 tablespoons cream
- 300 ml/½ pint/1¼ cups warm milk and water
- 1 tablespoon or 1 sachet instant dried yeast
- 2 teaspoons salt

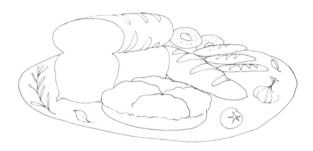

Mix the flour, yeast and salt together in a large bowl, or follow directions on the packet, using milk/water from the measured amount. Mix the eggs together with the cream and the remaining milk/water and pour into the centre of the flour. Mix with a wooden spoon or your hands, drawing in the flour from the sides until the dough holds together. If the dough is too dry, add a little water, a few drops at a time. Knead for 2 or 3 minutes (1 minute with a dough hook) until the dough becomes smooth and does not stick to your hands. Put the dough into an oiled bowl, cover with clingfilm and leave to rise in a warm place until doubled in bulk, about an hour.

Knock the air out of the dough, knead for a few moments, then shape into a long roll. Cut the roll into 16 equal pieces. Roughly flatten each piece into a circle and then roll up into a cylinder. Place each roll on a floured baking tray. Brush the tops lightly with beaten egg or cream and set aside for a further 20 minutes. Bake at 230°C/450°F/ Gas 8, lowering the heat after 10 minutes. Cook for a further 10–15 minutes, until nicely browned and giving a hollow sound when tapped underneath. Cool on a wire rack.

Note: This dough makes excellent pain au chocolate, real pain au chocolate, not to be confused with those sold in croissant shops, poor chocolate in greasy puff paste. The original idea was to combine good dark chocolate with plain bread dough. Try the above rolls with squares of Lindt's 70 per cent or similar chocolate wrapped inside. Bake as above. The chocolate stays put and the contrast is delicious.

BROWN YEAST BREAD

Another eighteenth-century bread, this time the type used for the household, when pure white bread was a luxury reserved for 'upstairs'.

The slightly longer rising time for this bread may seem like an obstacle, but it is really simple to make, keeps well and freezes excellently. It is worthwhile trying to find an organic stone-ground wholemeal for maximum flavour.

- 900 g/2 lb/7 cups coarse brown flour
- 1 tablespoon or 1 sachet instant dried yeast
- 750 ml/1¼ pints/3 cups warm milk and water
- 2 teaspoons salt

Put the flour into a mixing bowl with the yeast and salt, or follow directions on the packet, using water from the measured amount. Make a well in the centre and pour in the milk and water, holding back two or three tablespoons, and mix well with a wooden spoon, or dough hook if using a mixer, until all the flour is incorporated. Knead for 4–5 minutes by hand on a floured surface, about 2 minutes in a mixer. Oil the mixing bowl, turn the dough around in it, cover with clingfilm and leave to double in bulk, about 1 hour and 15 minutes.

Meanwhile prepare one 900 g/2 lb and one 450 g/1 lb loaf tin by rubbing with a little oil or butter.

When the dough has risen sufficiently knock it down and turn on to a floured surface. Knead again for a minute or two, then divide between the two tins. Cover with a damp tea towel and allow to rise for a further 20 minutes or until the dough rises to the top of the tin.

Bake at 220°C/425°F/Gas 7 for about 35–40 minutes until it is firm, slightly shrunk from the sides of the tin and gives a hollow sound when tapped underneath. Different flours and different ovens take slightly more or less time to cook, so check the bread after 25 minutes.

POTATO BREAD

A moist bread with an excellent texture and good keeping qualities. For a change try it with sun-dried tomatoes, herbs and olives.

- 100 g/4 oz/8 tablespoons cooked mashed potatoes
- 450 g/1 lb/4 cups strong white flour
- 1 teaspoon salt
- 1 tablespoon or 1 sachet instant dried yeast
- 300 ml/½ pint/1 cup water

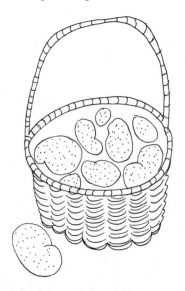

Boil the unpeeled potatoes in the usual way until tender, drain, cover with a tea towel and leave to dry for a few moments. Peel and mash the potatoes and push through a sieve.

Measure the flour into a mixing bowl, add the yeast, or follow directions on the packet, using water from the measured amount. Add the salt and rub the potato into the flour. Pour in the water and mix with a wooden spoon or dough hook until all the flour mixture is incorporated. Knead for 1 minute if using a mixer, or 3 or 4 minutes by hand. Transfer to an oiled bowl, cover with clingfilm or a tea towel and leave to rise until doubled in bulk, about 2 hours. It takes a little longer than usual.

Knock the dough back and knead for a few moments more, then shape into a rectangle and place in a 1 lb loaf tin. Leave to rise until it reaches the top of the tin.

Bake at 230°C/450°F/Gas 8 for about 25 minutes. To test, remove from the tin and tap the bottom of the loaf — if a hollow sound results, the loaf is cooked. Return the bread to the oven for 5 minutes to set the crust.

SAFFRON ROLLS

Delicious soft rolls with a golden colour and delicate saffron fragrance. Try baking some of the dough in dariole or castle pudding moulds for an attractive little shape to serve with soup or salads.

- 675 g/1½ lb/6 cups strong white flour
- 1 tablespoon or 1 sachet instant dried yeast
- 2 eggs
- 1 teaspoon sugar
- 1 good pinch saffron
- 1 teaspoon paprika
- 1 large tablespoon butter
- 150 ml/¼ pint/½ cup milk
- 150 ml/¼ pint/½ cup water
- 2 teaspoons salt
- egg yolk or cream for glaze

Put the flour and salt into a large mixing bowl. Sprinkle in the yeast or follow directions on the packet using the water and the sugar. Beat the eggs lightly. Warm the milk, put in the saffron and leave to infuse.

Make a well in the flour and pour in the eggs, milk and saffron, softened butter and yeast mixture. Mix together, drawing in the flour from the sides and adding 2–3 table-spoons or so of extra water if required. Knead until the dough is springy and elastic and not sticking to your hands. Turn into an oiled bowl, cover with a damp tea towel and leave to rise until doubled in bulk.

Knock back the dough and knead briefly on a floured sur-face, then shape into a long roll. Cut the roll into 16 equal pieces, shape into oval rolls and leave to rise again. Brush the tops lightly with the glaze and bake at 230°C/450°F/

Gas 8 for about 15 minutes, until a hollow sound results when tapped underneath.

If using dariole moulds, oil them first. A quarter of the above dough will be enough for 8–10 moulds, 5 cm high and 5.5 cm (2 x 2 ½ inches) wide. Half fill the moulds and allow to rise to the top before baking. Ten minutes should be enough to cook them. Brush with the glaze when cooked and return to the oven for 2 or 3 minutes.

OLIVE AND ONION BREAD

- 3 tablespoons chopped black olives
- 1 large Spanish onion, or 2 medium
- 675 g/1½ lb/6 cups strong white flour
- 425 ml/¾ pint/1½ cups water
- 1 tablespoon or 1 sachet instant dried yeast
- 2 tablespoons olive oil
- 1 teaspoon salt
- 4 vine tomatoes
- ½ teaspoon dried thyme or rosemary

Heat 2 tablespoons of olive oil in a heavy saucepan and cook the onions and tomatoes gently until the onions are transparent, the tomatoes reduced and their juice evaporated, about 20–30 minutes. Leave to cool slightly.

Put the flour, salt and yeast into a large mixing bowl, or follow the directions on the yeast sachet, using water from the measured amount. Make a well in the centre and pour in the tepid water with one tablespoon of olive oil. Work into the flour, gradually drawing in the flour from the sides and kneading until the dough is smooth and elastic, 2–3 minutes in an electric mixer with a dough hook, or 5–6 minutes by hand. Pour the cooled onion and tomato mixture, the herbs and the chopped olives into the bowl and knead into the dough until evenly distributed. This is a rather messy but nice job if being done by hand, a bit like making mud pies. Cornflour on your hands and work surface will help.

Put the dough into an oiled bowl, cover with clingfilm or a damp tea towel and allow to rise until doubled in bulk, about an hour or so.

Knock the air out of the dough and knead again briefly on a floured surface before shaping into a large oval loaf about 8–10 cm, 3–4 inches high, and tucking the edges underneath. Loaf tins, a 450 g/1 lb and a 900 g/2 lb, can be used if preferred.

Allow the dough to regain volume for about 20 minutes before baking at 230°C/450°F/Gas 8 for 10 minutes, then reduce the heat to 200°C/400°F/Gas 6 for a further 20 minutes or so. The bread is cooked when a hollow sound results when tapped underneath. If the bread has been baked in a tin, take it out of the tin and return it to the oven for about 5 minutes to crisp the crust. Stand or prop the loaf upright to cool.

RYE BREAD WITH CARAWAY SEEDS

Lovers of rye bread will know that with the exception of German pumpernickels and similar breads, all rye bread contains a proportion of wheat flour to enable it to rise. This recipe uses the batter method in which the yeast, liquid and wheat flour ferment together before adding the low gluten rye flour, producing a good light bread. Rye bread is at its best after a day or two and will keep for at least a week. Guinness enriches the rye flavour, but water can replace it if preferred.

- 225 g/8 oz/2 cups rye flour
- 100 g/4 oz/1 cup wholemeal flour
- 350 g/12 oz/3 cups strong flour
- 1 tablespoon or 1 sachet instant dried yeast
- 2 teaspoons salt
- 1 tablespoon sunflower seeds, optional
- 1 tablespoon caraway seeds
- 1 teaspoon sugar
- 450 ml/17 fl oz/1¾ cups mixed warm water and Guinness

Mix the white flour, seeds and salt together in a large mixing bowl. Sprinkle in the yeast (or prepare according to directions on the packet) using some of the measured water and the sugar. Pour the liquid into a well in the centre of the flour and mix all together with a wooden spoon or dough hook, drawing in the flour from the sides, and kneading until all the flour is incorporated. Cover with clingfilm and leave for about 45 minutes, until the batter has a slightly bubbly appearance.

Sprinkle in the rye flour gradually, mixing until all the flour is incorporated. If the dough is very stiff, a little more water may be needed, perhaps several tablespoonfuls, but add it gradually, kneading it in thoroughly until the dough is light and elastic and not too sticky. It will be easier to do this on a surface sprinkled with cornflour.

Cover the dough with clingfilm once again and leave to rise until almost doubled in bulk. Knock down the dough, knead it again for a few minutes and divide it between the oiled tins. For this quantity you will need a 450g (1 lb) and a 900g (2 lb) loaf tin. If you want the bread for sandwiches, use one 1–1.5 litre (3–3½ lb) tin. Stab the tops of the loaves here and there with a skewer to prevent cracks in the surface. Leave to rise again until the dough fills the tins, about 30 minutes or so.

Bake at 220°C/425°F/Gas 7 for about 15 minutes, lowering it for a further 20–30 minutes. A larger 3 lb loaf will take 10–15 minutes longer.

Turn the bread out of the tins and tap underneath — a hollow sound indicates they are cooked. Both tins will cook in much the same time. Turn off the oven and put the loaves back in on their sides for 5 minutes to finish the crust.

If you would like to have the shiny crust seen on bought rye bread, dissolve half an ounce of potato or rice flour in half a pint of boiling water and brush over the loaves before they go into the oven, and again halfway through the baking time.

BARLEY LOAF

In the northern regions of Europe, including Ireland, where wheat was a difficult crop, barley has been grown for centuries. In the past both breads and porridge made from this mellow grain were part of the daily diet. Nowadays it can be found in health food or specialist shops. Try using it for croûtes or crostini, toasted or fried in olive oil. The flavour is particularly good with the strongly flavoured Irish cheeses such as Ardrahan or Wexford Mature Cheddar.

- 200 g/6 oz/1¼ cups barley flour (meal)
- 425 g/14 oz/3¾ cups strong plain flour
- 1 tablespoon or 1 sachet instant dried yeast
- ¾ level tablespoon salt
- 1 teaspoon sugar
- 300 ml/½ pint/1 cup water
- 300 ml/½ pint/1 cup buttermilk or milk

Thoroughly mix the two flours together in a large bowl. Add the salt and the dried yeast and mix again, or follow directions on the yeast packet, using some of the measured liquid and the sugar. Make a well in the centre and pour in the water and buttermilk. Mix with a wooden spoon, drawing in the flour from the sides until all the flour in incorporated. Knead until a smooth dough is formed, one which will not stick to your hands, 2–3 minutes in mixer or 4–5 minutes by hand. Cover with a towel or clingfilm and leave in a warmish place until doubled in bulk, about an hour or more.

When ready to finish the bread, knock down the dough and knead again, folding and stretching it for a few minutes. Shape into a nice oval cushion, tucking the dough edges underneath. Put into a 900 g/2 lb loaf tin, or two smaller ones, or shape as a cob as in the preceding recipe. Bake at 220°C/425°F/Gas 7, then reduce to 200°C/400°F/Gas 6 after 15 minutes. The bread is ready if a hollow sound results when tapped underneath.

APRICOT AND WALNUT BREAD

- 75 g/3 oz/⅔ cup finely chopped dried apricots
- 75 g/3 oz/¾ cup roughly chopped walnuts
- 450 g/1 lb/4 cups strong white flour
- 75 g/3 oz/¾ cup coarse brown flour
- 1 tablespoon or one sachet instant dried yeast
- 325 ml/12 fl oz/1½ cups mixed milk and water
- 1 tablespoon olive oil
- 1 teaspoon salt

In a large mixing bowl mix together the flours, apricots, nuts, salt and dried yeast, or follow the directions on the yeast packet, using liquid from the measured amount.

Make a well in the centre and pour in the milk and water, kneading and drawing in the flour from the sides until it is all incorporated. Knead for 2 minutes with a dough hook or 5–6 minutes by hand on a floured surface. Oil the mixing bowl, put in the dough, cover with clingfilm and allow to rise until doubled in bulk, about 1 hour.

Knock the air out of the dough and knead briefly before turning out on to a floured surface. Shape into an oval about 200 x 130 x 85 mm (8 x 5 x 4 inches), tucking the edges underneath. Place on a floured baking tray, cover with clingfilm or a damp tea towel and leave to recover volume, about 20 minutes. Bake at 200°C/400°F/Gas 6 for about 30 minutes. Remove from the oven and tap underneath. If a hollow sound results, the bread is cooked. The bread can also be cooked in a 900 g/2 lb loaf tin.

SODA BREADS

PARMESAN SCONES

- 50 g/2 oz/4 tablespoons grated Parmesan or mature Cheddar
- 1 lb/450g/4 cups self raising flour
- 100 g/4 oz/ 8 tablespoons butter
- 1 egg
- 300 ml/½ pint/1¼ cups buttermilk
- 1 teaspoon salt
- egg yolk or cream to glaze

Heat the oven to 200°C/400°F/Gas 6. Sift the dry ingredients into a large bowl and rub in the butter. Mix in the grated cheese. Beat the egg into the buttermilk, then stir into the flour, lightly mixing with a fork until the milk is absorbed. An extra tablespoon or so of buttermilk may be needed. It is important to mix the dough lightly, handling as little as possible to keep the scones light.

Turn the dough out on to a lightly floured board and pat gently into a square. Cut into smaller squares, or use a scone cutter. Place the scones well apart on a greased baking sheet and bake for about 15–20 minutes at 200°C/400°F/Gas 6. The tops can be brushed with beaten egg or cream for a nice golden finish. Cool on a wire rack.

BUTTERMILK SODA LOAF

- 450 g/1 lb/4 cups plain white flour
- 50 g/2 oz/4 tablespoons butter
- ½ teaspoon salt
- ¼ teaspoon bicarbonate of soda
- 1 teaspoon baking powder
- 2 teaspoons sugar
- 1 egg, beaten
- 300 ml/½ pint/1¼ cups buttermilk
- 2 teaspoons caraway or cumin seeds, optional

Put the flour, sugar, seeds, salt, bread soda and baking powder into a large bowl and rub in the butter. Make a well in the centre of the flour and pour in the beaten egg and buttermilk, working lightly and quickly until a soft dough is formed, if necessary adding the remaining milk.

Turn out on to a floured board, shape into a high rectangular loaf, or use an oiled loaf tin. Make two diagonal cuts across the top and bake at 220°C/425°F/Gas 7 for 10 minutes, then reduce to 200°C/400°F/Gas 6 for a further 25 minutes approximately. Cool for 10 minutes or so before removing, if using a tin. Wrap in a clean tea towel and prop the bread upright to cool.

The same mixture can be shaped as scones and cooked either in the oven or on a hot griddle or heavy frying pan.

COURGETTE BREAD

This moist savoury bread is delicious with the courgette soup on page 48. This quantity gives a 450 g (1 lb) loaf, just enough for 6 good slices.

- 200 g/6 oz/1½ cups grated courgette
- 225 g/8 oz/2 cups plain flour
- 50 g/2 oz/4 tablespoons shelled pistachio nuts
- 1 teaspoon sugar
- ½ teaspoon ground cumin, or seeds
- ½ teaspoon chilli or cayenne
- 1 teaspoon baking powder
- 75 ml/3 fl oz/6 tablespoons light olive oil
- 2 eggs
- 2 fl oz water
- 1 level teaspoon salt

Put the grated courgette in a nylon sieve, sprinkle with the salt and leave to drain for 20 minutes.

Put the flour, nuts, sugar, baking powder and flavourings in a large bowl and mix well. Beat the eggs in a small bowl with the oil. Put the courgette into a tea towel, roll up and squeeze tightly to extract as much water as possible, then add to the flour etc. Fold the egg mixture into the flour and add sufficient water to make a fairly loose dough.

Turn the dough into an oiled loaf tin 16.5 x 10 x 7 cm (6.5 x 4 x 2.5 inches) and bake at 180°C/350°F/Gas 4 for 45 minutes. Test in the usual way by tapping underneath the loaf — if it gives a hollow sound it is ready.

WHOLEMEAL BROWN BREAD

A nutty and flavoursome brown bread which keeps well.

- 350 g/12 oz/2½ cups coarse wholemeal flour
- 175 g/6 oz/1 cup pinhead oatmeal
- 50 g/2 oz/¾ cup wheat germ
- 2 eggs
- approx. 425ml/¾ pint/1½ cups milk
- 2 tablespoons olive oil
- 2 teaspoons baking powder
- 1 teaspoon bread (baking) soda
- 1½ teaspoons salt
- 2 teaspoons sugar

Mix the dry ingredients together in a large mixing bowl. Put the lightly beaten eggs in a measuring cup, add the olive oil and make up to a pint with milk.

Make a well in the centre of the flour and pour in the milk mixture. Fold in the liquid quickly and thoroughly, incorporating all the flour, then turn into an oiled 900 g/2 lb loaf tin, smooth the top and make two diagonal cuts. Alternatively, put the dough on a lined baking sheet and shape into a round cake, making two cross cuts on top.

Bake at 220°C/425°F/Gas 7 for 15 minutes, then lower the heat to 190°C/375°F/Gas 5 for another 35–40 minutes. Check whether the bread is cooked by tapping on the bottom — if it sounds hollow, it's done. Remove from the tin immediately, wrap in a clean tea towel and prop upright until cool.

ROSEMARY, CARROT AND PISTACHIO SCONES

A savoury scone to eat with soup or salad.

- ½ teaspoon finely chopped rosemary
- 2½ tablespoons grated carrot
- 50 g/2 oz/½ cup pistachio walnuts
- 175 g/6 oz/1¾ cups wholewheat flour
- 175 g/6 oz/1¾ cups plain white flour
- 4 teaspoons baking powder
- 50 g/2 oz/4 tablespoons butter
- 2 large beaten eggs
- 150 ml/¼ pint/½ cup milk

Mix together the flours, baking powder and salt and rub in the butter. Add in the rosemary, carrot and pistachio. Make a well in the centre and add the beaten eggs and milk, mixing lightly and quickly to form a light dough. Roll or pat out 2 cm (1 inch) thick and cut into 5 cm (2 inch) squares or rounds and bake on a lined baking tray at 200°C/400°F/Gas 7 for 15–20 minutes. Serve warm.

Makes 10–12.

The carrot and rosemary can be replaced by grated unpeeled apple and mint.

Index